# Brilliant Internet for the Over 50s

## Microsoft® Windows Vista edition

## P.K. MacBride

Harlow, England • London • New York • Boston • San Francisco • Toronto • Sydney • Singapore • Hong Kong
Tokyo • Seoul • Taipei • New Delhi • Cape Town • Madrid • Mexico City • Amsterdam • Munich • Paris • Milan

**Pearson Education Limited**
Edinburgh Gate
Harlow
Essex CM20 2JE
England

and Associated Companies throughout the world

*Visit us on the World Wide Web at:*
www.pearsoned.co.uk

First published 2006
**Second edition published 2007**

ISBN: 978-0-132-35453-0

**British Library Cataloguing-in-Publication Data**
A catalogue record for this book is available from the British Library

10 9 8 7 6 5 4 3 2 1
11 10 09 08 07

Prepared for Pearson Education Ltd by Syllaba Ltd (http://www.syllaba.co.uk).
Typeset in 11pt Arial Condensed by 30
Printed and bound in Great Britain by Ashford Colour Press Ltd., Gosport.

*The publisher's policy is to use paper manufactured from sustainable forests.*

# Brilliant guides

## What you need to know and how to do it

When you're working on your computer and come up against a problem that you're unsure how to solve, or want to accomplish something in an application that you aren't sure how to do, where do you look? Manuals and traditional training guides are usually too big and unwieldy and are intended to be used as end-to-end training resources, making it hard to get to the info you need right away without having to wade through pages of background information that you just don't need at that moment – and helplines are rarely that helpful!

*Brilliant* guides have been developed to allow you to find the info you need easily and without fuss and guide you through the task using a highly visual, step-by-step approach – providing exactly what you need to know when you need it!

*Brilliant* guides provide the quick easy-to-access information that you need, using a table of contents and troubleshooting guide to help you find exactly what you need to know, and then presenting each task in a visual manner. Numbered steps guide you through each task or problem, using numerous screenshots to illustrate each step. Added features include 'See also...' boxes that point you to related tasks and information in the book, while 'Did you know?...' sections alert you to relevant expert tips, tricks and advice to further expand your skills and knowledge.

In addition to covering all major office PC applications, and related computing subjects, the *Brilliant* series also contains titles that will help you in every aspect of your working life, such as writing the perfect CV, answering the toughest interview questions and moving on in your career.

*Brilliant* guides are the light at the end of the tunnel when you are faced with any minor or major task.

## Publisher's acknowledgements

The author and publisher would like to thank the following for permission to reproduce the screen shots in this book:

Silver Surfers, Age-Net, Excite UK, Google UK, Uk Directory, UK Net Guide, Ask Jeeves, Is4Profit, Wikipedia, Web Museum, Project Gutenberg, Real, St Helens Chat, Slang Dictionary, 50 Connect, Tesco, Oxford Reference Online, RAC, Amazon UK, National Express, UK Index, the Civil War Image Map.

Microsoft product screen shot(s) reprinted with permission from Microsoft Corporation.

Every effort has been made to obtain necessary permission with reference to copyright material. The publisher apologises if, inadvertently, any sources remain unacknowledged and will be glad to make the necessary arrangements at the earliest opportunity.

## Author's acknowledgements

The author would like to thank Karen, Sally and Andy for making this project so enjoyable.

## About the author

P.K. MacBride spent 20 years at the chalkface in schools and technical colleges before leaving to work full-time as a writer, editor and typesetter. He has written over 100 books, mainly on computing topics, covering many aspects of computer programming, software applications and the Internet. He has been translated into over a dozen languages, including Russian, Portugese, Greek, Chinese and American.

# Contents

# Preface

When I was asked to write this book, I was not, at first, sure about the need for it. What's so special about the over 50s that they have to have their own guide to the Internet? I'm over 50 myself and I don't feel I'm different from an under 50. But then I thought about how I use the Internet now compared to how I used it when I was under 50 (trying to ignore the many developments over the last 10 years), and realised that things had changed. It's not the number of birthdays, as such, that make the difference, but the changes that happened while the years have been passing.

Under 50, you are more likely to have children at home and must take steps to try to protect them from unsuitable material that is all too present on the Internet; over 50, you won't have to worry about making sure that the parental controls are in place on your Internet browser – though you may need to set up grandparental controls! And with the children growing up, you may have more time – and if you are lucky – more money for your own leisure activities. (The Internet has been very useful there – it's a great place to book tickets, whether for films or flights, concerts or coaches!) Under 50, you probably have to focus much of your energy on your work; over 50 – and certainly over 60 – that pressure eases off and you have more time for friends and the wider family, which the years may have scattered. The Internet offers excellent ways to keep in close contact with those distant chums. Swift, simple, efficient email is the most obvious way, but not the only one – now you can even run a decent phone connection through the Internet and chat to cousin Gladys in Australia for as long as you like and at no extra cost. You can make new friends through the Internet too, and these may fill the space that work colleagues once held.

Under 50, you may shop online because you can get better prices or because you don't have the time to hike down to the high street. Over 50, and increasingly as we get older, the fact that someone else will lug the heavy shopping to the door becomes more of an attraction. And over 50, health issues, unfortunately, tend to figure rather larger in our lives, so we may make more use of the health information services and the support groups that operate online. I certainly found them useful while recovering from a heart attack (although I was under 50 at the time…).

But inside, whatever our age, we're still the same, aren't we? We still enjoy the same things, have the same interests, support the same teams; we still shop, take photos, have bank accounts, go on holidays, watch the news, send greetings to our loved ones, run clubs, play games, plan routes, listen to music, do crosswords and sometimes just plain want to know about stuff. So, if, dear reader, you are under 50, the bulk of this book might also be useful to you.

P.K. MacBride, *Southampton 2007*

# Introduction

Welcome to *Brilliant Internet for the Over 50s*, *Vista edition*, a visual quick reference book that shows you how to make the most of the rich resources available on the Internet. Focused specifically on the needs of those whose working life was not affected significantly by the web and email, it provides an introductory guide to communicating with old friends, seeking health advice, having groceries delivered, and much more…

## Find what you need to know – when you need it

You don't have to read this book in any particular order. We've designed the book so that you can jump in, get the information you need, and jump out. To find the information that you need, just look up the task in the table of contents, index, or Troubleshooting guide, and turn to the page listed. Read the task introduction, follow the step-by-step instructions along with the illustration, and you're done.

## How this book works

Each task is presented with step-by-step instructions in one column and screen illustrations in the other. This arrangement lets you focus on a single task without having to turn the pages too often.

# Step-by-step instructions

This book provides concise step-by-step instructions that show you how to accomplish a task. Each set of instructions includes illustrations that directly correspond to the easy-to-read steps. Eye-catching text features provide additional helpful information in bite-sized chunks to help you work more efficiently or to teach you more in-depth information. The 'For your information' feature provides tips and techniques to help you work smarter, while the 'See also' cross-references lead you to other parts of the book containing related information about the task. Essential information is highlighted in 'Important' boxes that will ensure you don't miss any vital suggestions and advice.

# Troubleshooting guide

This book offers quick and easy ways to diagnose and solve common problems that you might encounter using the Troubleshooting guide. The problems are grouped into categories that are presented alphabetically.

# Spelling

We have used UK spelling conventions throughout this book. You may therefore notice some inconsistencies between the text and the software on your computer which is likely to have been developed in the USA. We have however adopted US spelling for the words 'disk' and 'program' as these are becoming commonly accepted throughout the world.

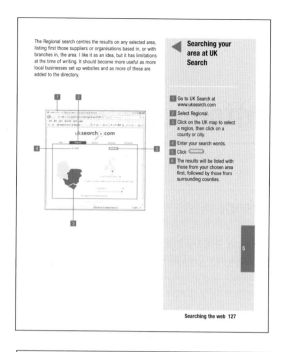

The Regional search centres the results on any selected area, listing first those suppliers or organisations based in, or with branches in, the area. I like it as an idea, but it has limitations at the time of writing. It should become more useful as more local businesses set up websites and as more of these are added to the directory.

**Searching your area at UK Search**

1 Go to UK Search at www.uksearch.com
2 Select Regional.
3 Click on the UK map to select a region, then click on a county or city.
4 Enter your search words.
5 Click .
6 The results will be listed with those from your chosen area first, followed by those from surrounding counties.

# Instant Internet

## Introduction

This is a largely practical chapter. Its aim is to show you how easy it is to find information on the World Wide Web, and to send and receive email messages.

To use this chapter, you need to have an Internet connection already in place, or if you haven't got one of your own yet, you need to visit one of the kids or a friend, or go to the public library – somewhere that you can get online.

I've tried to keep things as simple as possible, which hasn't been that difficult for me because the key Internet activities – surfing the web and sending email – are essentially quite simple. There are all sorts of refinements and alternative ways of achieving similar results, and there are a few complexities, but these can be ignored until you are ready to deal with them. Of course, this simplified approach does mean that if things go wrong – and they do from time to time – you may not know how to deal with it. But let's be positive. As long as you follow the instructions, you should be fine, and an hour or so from now, you should have visited half a dozen websites, and sent an email message.

Welcome to cyberspace!

# The Internet and the web

Let's start by clearing up a common misconception. The 'web' and the 'Internet' are not the same thing. Some people use the terms interchangeably, but they shouldn't.

- The **Internet** is the underlying framework. It consists of the computers, large and small, that store and process information for the Internet; the telephone wire, network cable, microwave links and other connections between them; and the software systems that allow them all to interact.

- The **World Wide Web** is the most visible and one of the simplest and most popular ways of using the net. It consists of – literally – billions of web pages, which can be viewed through browsers, such as Internet Explorer. The pages are constructed using HTML, that tells browsers how to display text and images, and how to manage links between pages. Clicking on a hypertext link in a page tells the browser to go to the linked page (or sometimes to a different type of linked file) – wherever it may be.

**Email** is another simple and very popular use of the Internet, and there are other more specialised Internet activities, as you will see later in this book.

## Jargon buster

**Browser** – application specially designed for accessing and displaying the information in the World Wide Web. This is also true the other way: the web is an information system designed to be viewed on browsers.

**Email** – electronic mail, a system for sending messages and files across networks.

**Net** – short for Internet. And Internet is short for interlinked networks, which is what it is. (See Chapter 2 for more details.)

**HTML** – HyperText Markup Language, a system of instructions that browsers can interpret to display text and images. HTML allows hypertext links to be built into web pages.

**Page** – or web page, a document displayed on the web. It may be plain or formatted text; and may hold pictures, sounds and videos.

**Web** – World Wide Web. Also shortened to WWW or W3.

Without further ado, let's go online and browse the World Wide Web. To do this you must first start Internet Explorer and connect to your Internet service provider.

You may find that when you start Internet Explorer, it will automatically try to make the connection. You may have to start the program and make the connection as two separate jobs. It all depends on your PC's setup – but either way, there's nothing difficult here, once you have located the icons on the Desktop or the Start menu.

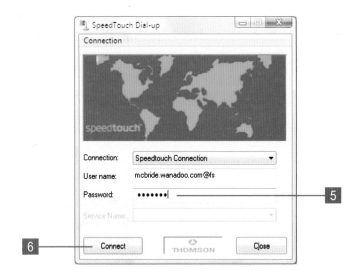

**1** Click the Internet Explorer item at the top of the Start menu, or

**2** Double-click the Internet Explorer icon on the Desktop.

**3** Wait a few moments for Internet Explorer to start.

**4** If Internet Explorer is set to connect to a website when it first starts, then the Connection dialogue box will appear automatically. If it does not, double-click the desktop icon for your Internet connection (mine is Speedtouch, yours may well be different.)

**5** The Connection dialogue box will have the User name already in place. The Password may also be there; if not type it in now.

**6** Click Connect .

**7** Wait a few seconds.

**Jargon buster**

**Browse** – move from one site to another on the web, enjoying the scenery and following up leads. Also called surfing.

# Discovering the Internet Explorer window

Internet Explorer, like most modern software, can be customised in many ways, so it's dangerous to say 'your screen should look like this…' because it may well not! Bearing this in mind, your Internet Explorer window should look like the one below – as long as you have all the toolbars open (and you will see how to do that in a minute), and as long as it's set to the same size (mine is a little over 900 by 700 pixels), and, of course, as long as you are at Internet Explorer's home page at Microsoft's website!

Title bar    Menu bar    Address bar    Standard toolbar    Links toolbar

?

## Did you know?

Internet Explorer is not the only browser. Netscape Navigator, Mozilla Firefox and Opera are all good alternatives. They are as powerful and as easy to use and are a little more secure and less troubled by viruses. The advantage of Internet Explorer is that it is already present in your computer. At some point, you might like to download and install one of these other browsers – they are all freely available on the Internet.

If you want to 'browse' the web, all you need is a good place to start, and one of the best places is a net directory – a site with sets of organised links to other sites. And one of the best directories is Yahoo! What makes it so useful is that it is extremely comprehensive, but all the sites listed there have been recommended by someone at some point. Quality control is rare on the web.

1 Go to the Yahoo! directory by typing this address into the Address bar: search.yahoo.com

2 Open the 'more' list and select Directory.

3 Think of a topic that interests you and in the web directory area click on the heading that the topic would fall under.

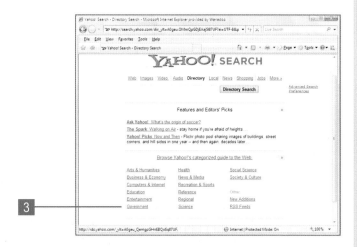

### Important

A hyperlink (link for short) is a connection to another web page. When you click on a link, Internet Explorer goes to that page and displays it. You know when you are on a link because the ⌖ pointer becomes a ⌐ hand.

## Browsing the web (cont.)

4 Use the category links to get down through two or three levels, to reach a specialised topic of your choice.

5 Click a Site listing link.

When you are looking for material at Yahoo! don't worry too much if you are not sure which category your topic will fit into. The directory is so well cross-referenced that any reasonable start point should get you there.

The directory is organised as a hierarchy with many levels. At each level there are three sets of links:

■ At the top are links to Categories – most of these are subdivisions of the current category; those with @ after the name are cross-links to other parts of the hierarchy.

■ The second set are Sponsored links – i.e. to firms that have paid to be included.

■ The third set are the Site listings.

As you work down through the levels, the first set shrinks, and the third set grows.

There's so much to see on the web! In fact, there's too much. You can often find links to scores – or even hundreds – of sites on a topic, so you have to learn to be selective or you can waste an awful lot of time online. Dip into a site to get an idea of what it is like, and if this is not really what you are looking for, move on and try elsewhere.

7

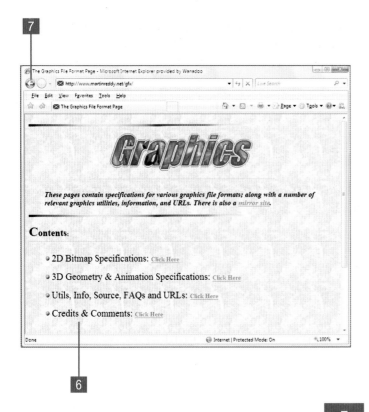

6

6 When the new page has loaded in, read to see if it is of interest. If you see a link that looks promising, click on it to find out where it leads.

7 If you want to go back to the previous page at the site, or back from there to Yahoo!, click ⬅.

8 If you want to start browsing a new topic, either work your way back to the start page in Yahoo!, or enter the search.yahoo.com address and start again from the top.

## Important

Sometimes when you click on a link, the new page opens in a new window. This can be useful as it means that the previous page is still there in the original Internet Explorer window. However, there are a couple of catches. It can get a bit confusing if you have too many windows open at once, and the Back button only works within the same window. As a general rule, if a site has opened in a new window, close the window when you have finished with that site.

# Searching the web

## Search the web

1. Go to Google at:
   www.google.co.uk

2. Type in one or more words to describe what you would like to find, e.g. 'bayeux tapestry', or 'bridge club bradford'.

3. If you are looking for an organisation or supplier in the UK, or you want information about something UK-based, select the pages from the UK option.

4. Press the [Enter] key or click the ⌈ Google Search ⌋ button.

5. The results show the names and the first couple of lines of details from the matching pages. Scroll through to find the ones that look most promising.

6. Click on the page name link to go to the page.

7. Use ⟵ to return to Google if you want to follow up other links.

Web directories offer one approach to finding material on the web. Search engines offer another, and this is often the best way if you are looking for very specific information. A search engine is a site that has compiled an index to web pages, and which lets you search through the index. There are several dozen search engines, and they compile their indices in different ways and to different levels of completeness, but some of the best know what's on 80% or more of the pages on the web. The most complete and the most effective is Google. It is so well used and loved that searching the web is now often called 'googling'.

You search by giving one or more words to specify what you are looking for. Try to be specific. If you search for 'football', 'bridge' or 'gardening' you will get millions of links to possible pages.

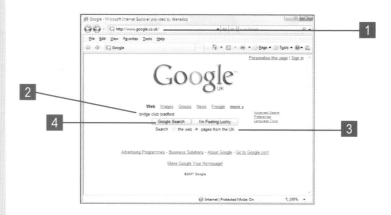

Google has links to over 8 billion pages in its index! Which is why you have to be as specific as possible when looking for particular information. However, sometimes it pays to be less specific, as this can produce leads that you might never have thought of yourself.

It doesn't matter too much if you get millions of results from a search as the good stuff tends to be listed at the top. (Google has developed some very clever systems for rating pages.)

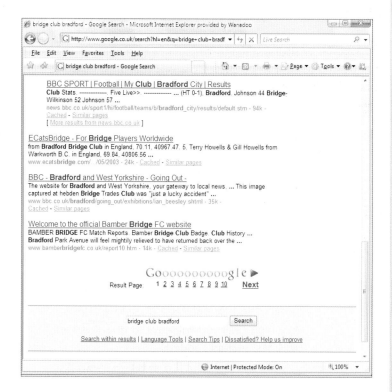

## Important

You will find a link to the next page at the bottom of the results listing, but as a general rule, if you don't see anything useful in the first page, subsequent pages are unlikely to be any better. Try a new search, with different words.

# Learning about email

The World Wide Web may well be the most glamorous aspect of the Internet and the one that grabs newcomers, but email is the aspect that many people find the most useful in the long run. It is quick, reliable and simple to use.

- Email is quick. When you send a message to someone, it will normally reach their mailbox within minutes – and usually within half an hour. However, it will only be read when the recipient collects the mail, and that may be anything from a few minutes later to when they get back from holiday.

- Email is reliable. As long as you have the address right, the message is almost certain to get through. And on those rare occasions when it doesn't, you will usually get it back with an 'undeliverable' note attached.

- Email is simple to use. You can learn the essential skills in minutes – as you will see very shortly!

## Email addresses

Email addresses vary hugely, but take the general form:

name@service.provider

Where 'name' identifies the person, and may be their full name, or name with initials, or the name with a number afterwards (because there is often more than one John Smith or Mary Jones with the same service provider).

'service.provider' is usually the name of the organisation through which a person gets their email, e.g. **btinternet.com**.

There are lots of variations, and you must get the address exactly right – there is no postie to guess what you mean. To start communication with other people, you ask them for their address, and double-check the spelling and punctuation, or get them to send you an email – in which case you will have to give them your address, just as carefully.

We will take a closer look at addresses in Chapter 8.

## Did you know?

If you have a dial-up connection, where you pay for the time you spend online, email can be the cheapest use of the Internet – and the cheapest form of communication of any kind (apart from a natter over the back fence). Messages can be read and written offline, so you only need to be online while you send and receive them. As text travels very swiftly over the Internet you should find that you can send and receive the day's messages in less than a minute.

Windows Mail is currently the most widely used email software among private users. (People working for businesses or other organisations are more likely to use the email software in the Outlook suite.)

Windows Mail is very simple to use. You can pick up your mail with one click of a button. It takes a little more to send a message, but there's nothing complicated in it.

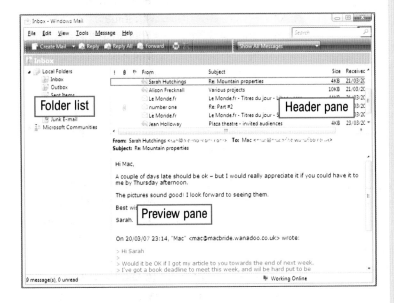

Folder list

Header pane

Preview pane

**1** Start Windows Mail from the Start menu.

**2** Identify the marked areas. If you are working on a friend's PC, check before you read any messages! If it's your own PC, and the software has been installed recently, you should have a welcome message from Microsoft.

### Important

Your Windows Mail display may contain more elements than this – I have turned off all the non-essential parts. You will find out how to customise the display in Chapter 9.

# Reading an email message

When messages arrive, they are dropped into the Inbox folder. Opening them for reading is very straightforward. After reading, you can reply if you like, and the messages can be deleted or you can move them to another folder – you might want to keep some for future reference. You can also just leave the messages in the Inbox for the time being.

1 Start Windows Mail, and select Inbox in the Folder list, if necessary.

2 Click anywhere on a message's line in the Header pane to open the message in the Preview pane.

After reading the message...

3 If you don't want it any more, click Delete.

4 If you want to leave it in the Inbox for the time being, click on the header line of the next message to read that.

5 If you want to respond to it, click Reply – and we will continue this on page 14.

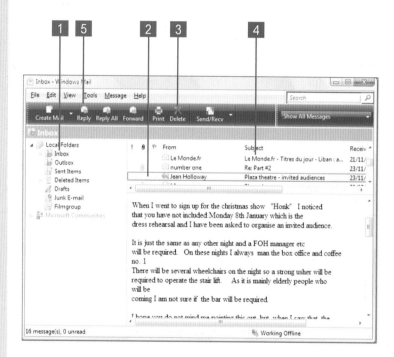

If you want to respond to it, click Reply – and we will continue this on page 14.

## For your information

Windows Mail is not the only email application. If you have Microsoft Office, then you will have Outlook – its big brother! (This does far more than email, but if email is all you want, Mail is a better product.) Netscape includes a good email application in its package of Internet tools.

To send an email message, all you need is an address to write to and something to say – although even that is not absolutely essential. For practice right now, ask a friend for their address, or if there is no one conveniently at hand, send the message to me at: macbride@tcp.co.uk

Writing an email is not as formal as writing a letter. You do not need to put the date or your address on the message – they will both be added automatically when it is sent. Good spelling also seems to be optional, judging by the messages I receive – even though most email software now has a Spelling button.

1 Open the Message menu and select New Message, or click the Create Mail toolbar button.

   When the New Message window opens, you will see that it has lots of features. You only need to deal with four of them – ignore the rest for now.

2 Click into the To: field and type the address of the person you want to send the message to.

3 Click into the Subject: field and type a few words describing what the message is about. This is not essential, but your recipients will appreciate it, as it will help them to deal with their email efficiently.

4 Click into the working space and type your message.

5 Click Send.

# Sending your messages

If you are online, the message may be sent immediately, or later, depending upon the optional settings (see page 196).

If you are offline, it will be stored in the Outbox folder, ready for sending next time you connect to your online mailbox.

1  If you are not online, go online now.

2  Open the Tools menu, point to Send and Receive then select Send and Receive All or click the Send/Recv button.

3  A progress indicator box will usually open. After a short delay you should see the indicator moving across the bar – though a short message will normally travel so quickly that you'll scarcely have time to see the indicator moving.

4  If you have had any new messages, there will be a number in brackets after the Inbox name. Click on the Inbox to open it, then click on a message in the Header pane to read it.

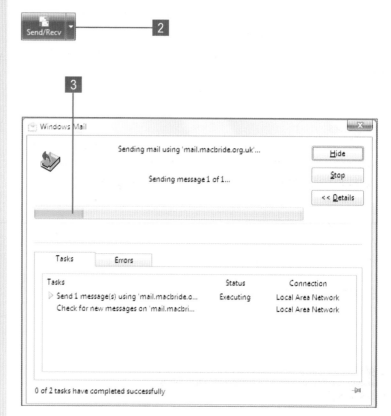

With a broadband connection, it costs you nothing to leave the line open all the time that you are at the computer – so that you can pick up or send mail, or look something up on the web whenever you want. You only need to end the connection when you close down the computer.

With a standard dial-up connection, it is a different matter altogether. When you are online you may be paying for the cost of the phone call (or not, it depends upon the nature of your service contract) but you are certainly tying up the telephone line. You should end the connection as soon as you have finished working online.

You should close the connection properly – don't just close the browser or Windows Mail. This ensures that you are properly disconnected from your service provider's computer.

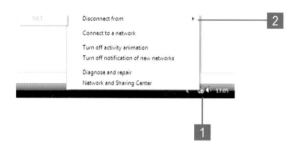

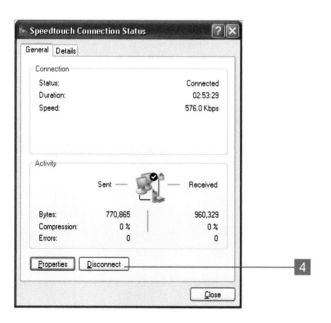

## End your online session

1 Right-click  in the Taskbar tray (next to the clock).

2 Point to Disconnect from the pop-up menu, and select Connection.

or

3 If the connection button
Speedtouch Con... is present on the Taskbar, click it to bring the Connection status dialogue box into view.

4 Click Disconnect .

# Internet FAQs

## Introduction

FAQ stands for Frequently Asked Questions. On many Internet sites you will find an FAQ list of questions and their answers. If you ever need help at any site, always look first for the FAQs before you ask someone for help – it is better than bothering the site's staff unnecessarily and, in any case, it will be far quicker than waiting for a reply.

Take the time now to read through this chapter before you start to go online. If you understand – at least in general terms – the key concepts and jargon of the Internet and the World Wide Web, what it's all about and how it fits together, then you will find it easier to learn the software and the techniques that you need for actually doing anything on the net.

## What you'll cover

**What is the Internet?**

**How did the Internet start?**

**Where did the web come from?**

**How are web pages created?**

**What's in a page?**

**What is a hyperlink?**

**Can I have my own website?**

**What's in a website address?**

**What's a URL?**

**How does email work?**

**Is email safe?**

**What does an email address look like?**

**What are newsgroups?**

**How can I meet people online?**

**What can I download from the web?**

**What do I need to get online?**

**How do I choose an ISP?**

# What is the Internet?

Networks bring people, information and resources together. On any network – including the Internet – the users can communicate with each other and share their data files if they want to. On an office network, the users can also share the printers, modems, disk drives and other resources attached to the computers on the network.

The Internet is a set of **inter**connected **net**works – hence the name – which links millions of computers throughout the world. The networks vary greatly in the number of computers that are connected to them, and in the way that they are organised. Some are limited to a single office, others join distant sites and may link an organisation's offices in different cities or even in different countries. The networks are owned by businesses, universities, governments and other organisations. Some exist mainly to provide internal communications and shared services for the organisation's own employees and users; but those run by Internet service providers (ISPs) are there so that members of the public and smaller businesses can get access to the Internet.

The networks are linked through public or private phone lines, which may run over cable or via microwave links. At first, these connections were mainly used for voice communications, and the Internet was just thumbing a ride, but as the Internet has grown, new cable and microwave connections have been built specifically for the net, to cope with the increasing heavy traffic. The computers that are linked through these networks vary from giant supercomputers down to desktop machines – mainly PCs and Apple Macs.

## Jargon buster

**Domain name** – the part of an Internet address that identifies the organisation that it belongs to.

**Internet service provider** – organisation whose main business is to enable people to access the Internet.

## Important

The Internet has no central governing body, though the Internet Society provides some coordination and InterNIC (the Network Information Center) controls the allocation of domain names. There are also technical and regional bodies which coordinate the activities of service providers and other organisations. The Internet relies on cooperation, driven by goodwill and enlightened self-interest. It generally works, but there are disadvantages. There is no quality control on the net so there's a certain amount of rubbish out there; and it is difficult to prevent antisocial and criminal activity.

The Internet story starts in the late 1960s when the US government's Advanced Research Project Agency was asked to develop a long-distance communications network that would be robust enough to withstand nuclear attack. It came up with ARPAnet which linked four computers in different places in the USA. What made the ARPAnet system robust was the fact that it was multi-connected and data travelled around it in small blocks or 'packets'. This system is still used. Each packet is labelled with its origin, destination and position in the stream of data. The safe receipt of each packet is acknowledged, so that both ends of the connection know how the transmission is going. If a packet doesn't get through, it is re-sent. If the connection between any two nodes is broken (or bombed, in the original scenario), it will re-establish itself via an alternative route, and any packets of data that didn't reach their destination will be sent again along the new route.

From those initial four computers, the net grew slowly over the next 10 years to connect around 200 computers and networks in military and research establishments within the USA, plus a few overseas links. It proved, beyond doubt, the practicality and benefits of inter-networking. By the mid-1980s several academic and research inter-networks had been set up. These combined with ARPAnet to form the basis of the Internet.

The growth of the Internet has been phenomenal. One of the most accurate measures of its size is the count of host computers. In 1990, there were around 150,000 host computers; 10 years later, there were almost 100 million, and at the time of writing, the number is over 450 million.

The number of people with access to the Internet has grown at a similar pace. From around 1 million in 1990, it had risen to nearly 50 million by 1995, and on to 400 million by 2005. The best estimates today put the number at nearly 1,000 million, but it looks like the boom is beginning to tail off. This is hardly surprising. In most developed countries, most people who want access to the Internet now have it, and have been connected for a few years.

# How did the Internet start?

## Timesaver tip

The multi-connection, packet-based system has stood the test of time. Even when natural disaster or human error knocks out part of the network, connections can normally be made through alternative routes – and it is worth remembering that there are always alternative routes. Sometimes you may have difficulty downloading a page from a site simply because there is a 'traffic jam' at some point along the route. If you stop the download and access the site afresh, your system may find a different and faster route.

## Jargon buster

**Host computer** – one that is permanently connected to the Internet and which provides storage space for files that others can access, or manages email or offers some other service.

# Where did the web come from?

One reason why the growth of the Internet was relatively slow at first was that it was hard to use. There were three main activities:

- **Telnet** – running programs on a distant computer, something purely for the techies.
- **File transfer** – downloading documents and files from special file stores. The techies enjoyed that as well, and quite a few non-technical academics learnt how to do it because there were some valuable research materials in those stores.
- **Email** – which has always been quite simple to use, but alone was not enough to bring many people online.

The first attempt at making information accessible to the non-technical user was Gopher. This failed as it relied on cataloguing. If you wanted to add a document to the system, someone somewhere had to catalogue it. And it all relied on volunteer labour. Gopher got off the ground, but it never flew. At its height, it encompassed only several hundred thousand documents.

It was a British scientist, Tim Berners-Lee, who came up with the answer – the World Wide Web. This is based on hyperlinks, which are connections between documents. A hyperlink has two parts: some text or an image which (generally) indicates what is linked, and the Internet address of the linked document. If you view a hyperlinked document in a browser, when you click on a linked text or image, the browser will access the linked document, and display it.

The beauty of the web, and the reason for its rapid growth, was its simplicity – both for its users and for the people putting information onto it. Browsers are simple to use, and it is simple enough to create documents and to put them onto the web. There is no cataloguing, and therefore no need to wait for anyone's permission to open your web pages to the world. You can connect all your own documents using hyperlinks, and advertise the address of your site in the press, or in academic articles or simply by emailing your friends and colleagues. If people find your site useful, they will add links to it on their sites – which will be linked from other people's, and so on.

The first website was opened in December 1990. A year later there were ten sites, and the year after that there were fifty. Slow growth? Yes, but this was still experimental. By 1994 there were 10,000 websites; by 1998 there were 1 million; 10 million by 1999; and almost 100 million today. And those 100 million sites now contain over 8 billion documents!

Web pages can be produced in two distinct ways: they can be created by a person and saved as a file, or they can be created – on demand – by a program, so that the page meets the visitor's needs. The program draws from a database the required information, e.g. the details of a book, and adds HTML tags to make it display as required.

All web pages are written in HTML (HyperText Markup Language) which defines how and where text and images appear. A simple HTML file looks like this:

```
<HTML>
<HEAD>
<TITLE>My French home page</TITLE>
</HEAD>
<BODY>
<H2>My French home page</H2>
<IMG SRC = "view.jpg">
<P>My favourite view.</P>
</BODY>
</HMTL>
```

And produces this display:

**<TITLE>My French home page<TITLE>**
Set the title page

**<H1>My French home page<H1>**
Sets the text in Heading 1 style

**<IMG SRC = "view.jpg">**
Displays the image

**<P>My favourite view.<P>**
Starts a new Paragraph

## Important

If a page is an HTML file, it can be viewed again when you are not online (page 251) and can be saved (page 250). These are not possible if it has been created by a program. You can tell what sort of page it is by looking carefully at the Address bar. If the filename includes '.htm' or '.html', then it is an HTML file. If it includes '.asp' or 'php', then the page has been created by a program – ASP and PHP are the two languages most commonly used for creating web pages.

# What's in a page?

Typically, a web page will consist of several different files. The main file holds the text and the coding that tells the browser what to display and where. Each image is a separate file and there may be other files for music or special effects. These files must be downloaded before they can be displayed.

Pages can be put together in a number of ways, and the construction affects how they download and are displayed.

- A simple page will display the text as soon as it downloads, then show the images one by one as they arrive.

- Some pages are built using tables, which give better control over layout. Browsers normally wait until all the table's data has arrived before they display any of it. You may see nothing at first and then the whole page suddenly appears.

Table-based page – here the layout table divides the page into three columns, below the heading area.

- Some pages use frames. These divide the screen into two or more areas, and allow part of the display to be changed while the rest remains static. Framed pages download in sections, but you will usually get one section quickly.

Navigation frame with links to all areas of the website

Header frame – keeps a few links always in view

Display frame – items selected in the navigation frame are displayed here

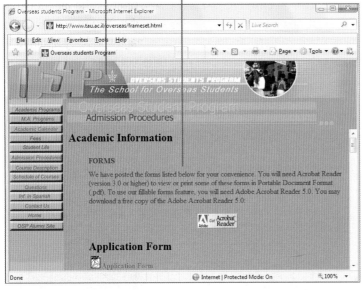

Framed page – note the scroll bars on the lower right frame

**See also**

Printing web pages, page 68, which looks at how to print framed pages.

# What is a hyperlink?

Hyperlinks are what make the web what it is, and what make it so easy to use. Without them, you would have to know – and type in correctly – the address of every page that you wanted to visit. Surfing would be a slow, tedious business, and you would spend more time looking up addresses in reference books than visiting pages! Instead of all this, you just click a link to go to the linked page.

Hypertext links can be attached to text or images. The text may be an item in a list, or a word or phrase within a paragraph. If text is hyperlinked, it will be displayed with an underline and in a different colour (usually blue, but this can be changed).

Images can be linked in two ways. At the simplest, the whole image carries a single link. In this case, the image will normally have a blue outline. An image can also be set up as an image map, with different parts carrying different links.

Whether hyperlinks are in text, images or image maps, there is a simple way of recognising them. When you place the screen pointer over a hyperlink, it chages from an arrow ⇖ to a hand 🖑.

**To see maps related to the movie <u>click here</u>.**
Hyperlinked text is underlined.

Links on an image map – an image where each area carries a different link. In this case, the image map is of a map!

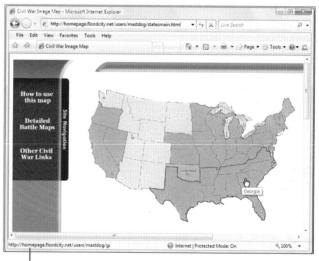

When you point to a link, the address of the page appears here

24

You certainly can! Anyone can create a site and publish their own pages on the World Wide Web. Most ISPs offer a web hosting service to their members. Many also offer tools for creating web pages and building a site, though these are not really necessary. As long as you don't want 'bells and whistles' and flashy effects, it is not difficult to create attractive, illustrated web pages.

People use their websites for many things. For example, to:

- Run a club or society, publicising contact details, events calendar, reports of meetings, etc.

- Tell the world about their hobby – and these sites can be invaluable sources of information.

- Keep distant family and friends informed, showing the latest photos and movie clips. The fact that no one outside of the circle will be interested doesn't matter – you do not have to have lots of people visiting your site.

- Publish their own writing, poetry or artworks.

- Advertise their products or services – people have grown small websites into big businesses.

People use their websites for all sorts of reasons, and produce all manner of results. Some, like this angling-centred site of David Lawton, are interesting and beautifully presented. Go see for yourself at: www.geocities.com/davyravy2000

**Jargon buster**

**Web host** – organisation that provides a web address and the space to store the files, so that people and smaller firms can set up their own websites.

# What's in a website address?

Every computer site that is linked to the internet has its own unique address. This normally begins www to show that it is on the World Wide Web, and is followed by the domain name. This has two or more parts, separated by dots, e.g.:

**www.virgin.co.uk**

The first part of the domain name identifies the organisation, and is based on its name – this one is of the Virgin company.

The next part identifies the nature of the organisation. (This can be omitted.) The most common ones are:

| | |
|---|---|
| com | commercial (USA and international) |
| co | commercial (outside the USA) |
| edu | educational (USA) |
| ac | academic (outside the USA) |
| net | network provider |
| gov | government department |
| mil | military |
| nhs | hospital or other NHS facility (UK) |
| org | non-commercial organisation |

At the right-hand end is the country code. This is omitted for US-based and international organisations. Examples are:

| | | | |
|---|---|---|---|
| au | Australia | ca | Canada |
| co | Colombia | do | Dominican Republic |
| fr | France | fi | Finland |
| de | Germany | hk | Hong Kong |
| ie | Ireland | in | India |
| it | Italy | jp | Japan |
| tv | Tuvalu | uk | United Kingdom |

The country code is usually a good guide to the location of the organisation, but people can register in another country. You can get cool names that way! **buy.it** and **sell.it** have already gone, as have other Italian names that produce English phrases. The tiny island state of Tuvalu has done very nicely out of selling **.tv** addresses to television companies!

## Important

Not all website addresses start with www. Alternative starts may indicate the type of facility at the site, e.g. **search** or **mail**, or may indicate that the site is so large it has had to be split up over several computers, e.g. **www2**. If you are copying an address, never assume anything!

With so many millions of web pages, files, newsgroups and email addresses that can be reached over the internet, a standardised and systematic way of identifying them is essential. URLs – Uniform Resource Locators – provide this.

There are different styles of URL for each approach to the Internet, though they all follow much the same pattern:

**type://host computer/folder/filename**

## Web page URLs

Many of these are instantly recognisable from their html or htm endings, which shows that they are hypertext pages.

**http://www.sus-uk.com/individuals/waste/composting.html**

This one is a page with advice on composting, at the Sustainable UK (sus-uk) website (www).

On larger commercial sites, web pages are often generated automatically from information held in databases. If you have 1,000 products or 2,000,000 book and CD titles, it is far more efficient to produce pages this way than to have to create a separate page for each product and arrange all the pages in some kind of catalogue. You can often recognise these pages by their .php or .asp endings – these indicate the programming language, ASP or PHP, used to produce them.

**http://www.tickets.eno.org/daily_events_list.asp**

This is where you can buy tickets for English National Opero (eno) performances.

A web URL does not have to include a page name:

**http://homepages.tcp.co.uk/~macbride**

Here's my home page, in case you want to drop by. Like the URLs of many personal home pages, this consists of the address of a computer at my service provider, followed by a tilde (~) and my user name.

The URL of the top page of a site may just consist of the site address, with an (optional) slash at the end. This will take you to the opening page at Microsoft's site.

**http://www.microsoft.com/**

# What's a URL?

**2**

## Important

The URLs of web pages can sometimes be very complex, making typing them in a real chore. Fortunately, you rarely have to do this more than once – if at all – as browsers can capture and store addresses in several ways. Look out for the AutoComplete facility (page 44), Favourites (page 47) and History (page 56).

# How does email work?

It may help you to have an overview of the technology behind email, so you can use it more efficiently and are less likely to get fazed when things don't quite go according to plan!

When you send an email message, it does not go direct to your recipient, as a phone call does. Instead it will travel through perhaps a dozen or more computers before arriving at its destination – in the same way that snail mail passes through several post offices and depots. The message goes first to the mail server at your ISP. This will work out which computer to send it to, to help it towards its destination. The server will normally hold the message briefly, while it assembles a handful of messages to send to the next place – in the same way that a post office sorts and bags its mail. Each mail server along the way will do the same thing, bundling the message with others heading in the same direction. This method gives more efficient Internet traffic and at the cost of very little delay – most messages will normally be delivered in less than an hour.

However, your recipients won't necessarily be reading the message within the hour. The delivery is to their mail boxes at their service providers. People only get their email when they go online to collect it. (Though with a broadband account and automated collection it can feel as if its delivered.)

Email messages are sent as text files. Delivery time for plain text message will normally be very short, as it takes only one byte to represent a character – (plus about 10% more for error-checking). A ten-line message, for example, will make a file of around 1 Kb, and that can be transmitted in about three seconds. Images, video clips and other files can be sent by mail (see page 206) but they must first be converted into text format. You don't need to worry about how this is done, as Windows Mail will do all the conversion automatically. What you do need to know is that conversion increases the size of files by around 50%, so even quite small images can significantly increase the time it takes to send or receive messages.

## Jargon buster

**Error-checking** – the techniques used to make sure that data sent over the Internet arrives intact. If a block of data is damaged, it is sent again.

**ISP** (Internet service provider) – the company that supplies your connection to the Internet.

**Mail server** – computer that stores and handles email.

**Plain text** – text without any layout or font formatting.

**Snail mail** – hand-delivered by the postman.

The short answer is 'yes – as long as you are careful.' There are two potential sources of problems, spam and viruses.

Spam (named after the famous Monthy Python sketch) is junk mail – unsolicited emails sent out in huge numbers. Some offer cheap products, mainly mortgages, loans, medications (especially of Viagra and the like) and software (probably pirated). How many actually supply the goods after taking your money is unknown, but I suspect it is none and I'm not wasting my money by testing it. No reputable firm uses spam to advertise its products. A lot of spam comes from sites selling sex in various forms – apparently pornography is currently the most profitable business on the web. Some spams are cons, either hidden in what seems to be a request from your bank for you to check your details 'for security reasons', or offering a share of some dodgy cash if you will help to get it out of the con man's country – typically Nigeria. Amazingly, some people still fall for these. Finally, there is the type of spam that seems innocuous, such as an invitation to take part in a survey, but is actually building a list of email addresses to sell to other spam merchants.

There is only one safe thing to do with spam: delete it without opening it. Spam messages may link back to a website to download images, but once you are linked to that site it may be able to identify your computer and to access it.

A virus is a malicious program that sneaks onto your computer and then tries to spread to others. They can be hidden in other programs, such as games and screensavers, that are offered for free downloading from the internet. They can also be hidden in email attachments, and in fact this is how most viruses are propagated these days. Once they have got onto a computer, they will typically go through its address book and send themselves to all the contacts with a covering email saying something to the effect 'I thought you might like to see this'. They can do real damage to your system, deleting or corrupting files.

Files which can contain viruses include any kind of program and documents which may have macros (a kind of program) embedded in them. To avoid viruses, never open any attachment in an email from anyone that you do not know, and any unexpected ones from people that you do know. Don't worry about family snaps – photographs (.jpg files) and movie clips (.avi, .mpg, .mpv, .wmv and similar files) are safe.

## Is email safe?

2

**! Important**

Viruses are difficult to remove so make sure you keep them out by installing antivirus software and keeping it up to date. AVG Antivirus is one of the leading free antivirus software solutions. Download a copy from **avg.antivirus-home.com**.

**See also**

Read Checking the Security options, page 85, for more on keeping your email safe.

## What does an email address look like?

### Jargon buster

**Site address** – the identifier of the website. This will be a main part of the addresses of pages at that site or of people who get their email through the site.

The basic pattern for an email address is:

**name@site.address**

Notice the punctuation – an @ sign after the name, and dots between the constituent parts of the site address. Now, while addresses follow simple rules and are fairly easy to remember, you cannot work them out for yourself and you must get them exactly right.

The **name** is usually based on the person's real name, though how it is formed varies. If the person works for an organisation, its IT service will probably have rules for creating names. Someone who gets online through an ISP, or has a web mail account, will have more choice over their name, but even here there will be some constraints. For example, the name for 'Johnny B. Goode' might be 'jbgoode', 'johnnyg', 'John?_Goode', 'johnny.b.goode', 'goode3' or other variations.

Notice that both _ and . are used for punctuation, and that sometimes a number will be added, especially to common names.

The simplest form of **site address** is the domain name of the organisation that is providing the mail service. For example, I have a dial up account at TCP (which stands for Total Connectivity Providers and is nothing to do with antiseptic lotions). Their domain name is tcp.co.uk, and the name that they allocated to me was:

**macbride@tcp.co.uk**

Sometimes the site address also includes a part to identify the account. This is used where the service allows several people to have email addresses on the one account. For example, I also have a broadband account with Wanadoo, and my site address there is:

**@macbride.wanadoo.co.uk**

And a different name is tacked at the front of this for each family member that uses this service.

Newsgroups are the electronic equivalent of the letters pages in newspapers. People will send in their 'articles' – perhaps thoughts on a current issue or a request for information – and others may respond to these. Controversial topics can often stimulate long exchanges of sometimes heated views. The software groups articles and their responses into 'threads', so that others can follow the exchanges.

There are literally thousands of newsgroups, each dedicated to a specialist topic, ranging from intense academic and technical debates through to the truly frivolous, with all manner of esoteric, exotic and erotic topics in between.

They are text-based and are normally accessed through email software, but the articles are not sent out like email. When you link to a group, only the headers (containing the names of the senders, the subjects and dates) are downloaded at first. The bodies of the messages are only downloaded if you choose to read them.

Some newsgroups are public, so that anyone can read the articles or send in their own contributions; others are restricted to members – though membership is usually free and open to any interested party.

Some newsgroups are 'moderated' – they have someone who reads the articles and filters out those which are off-topic, irrelevant or otherwise not worth circulating. Most are unmoderated, and these are either a free, open and democratic exchange of views or a terrible 'waste of bandwidth'. It depends upon the group and on your own viewpoint.

Newsgroups can be excellent resources. It is well worth spending a little time sifting through them to find the gems that appeal to you. You'll see how in Chapter 10.

# What are newsgroups?

## Jargon buster

**Bandwidth** – strictly refers to the capacity of the phone line, but is also used to refer to other transmission and storage resources. If someone describes your email or your website as being a 'waste of bandwidth', they didn't think much of it!

# How can I meet people online?

You can meet people online in a variety of ways – it depends upon what sort of people you want to meet, and why.

- **Discussion groups**, or forums, are good places to meet new people who share your interest in a particular hobby, activity or subject, though 'meet' is not quite the right verb. In the groups, the discussion is by posting and replying to messages. Sometimes several people will be online at the same time and the exchanges will be almost immediate, but more often there can be quite a time lapse between messages. In some groups it is possible to establish direct email contact with other members, and real friendships can develop. The groups can also be a good way to organise and advertise real world events.

Places like Yahoo, Google and other big directory sites host large numbers of discussion groups covering a huge range of topics. But note that the level of activity and the quality of the discussions vary greatly, and it can take a while to find a group where you feel at home.

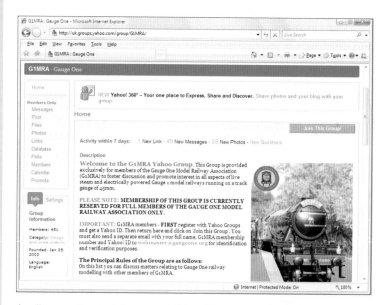

A railway enthusiasts' group at Yahoo! To explore Yahoo! groups, go to uk.yahoo.com and click the Groups link in the list of options on the left of the page.

- In **chat rooms**, the interaction is in real-time. People communicate by typing, with all the inputs appearing on the screen as they are received. If more than two people are interacting at the same time, the lines of 'chat' get intermingled and it can be quite difficult to follow a thread or to make your point. In the general, open-access, chat rooms the quality of conversation is indescribably poor – about what you would expect when strangers meet in an unstructured environment. However, the chat room sites also offer private rooms were friends can arrange to meet and have a proper discussion.

- If you are searching for **friends**, old or new, there are plenty of online facilities. For re-establishing old contacts, Friends Reunited is the leading service in the UK, with around 12 million people in its database at the time of writing. Its existence has lead to an increase in better-attended school reunions, and it has been cited in not a few marriage breakups as people have met up and gone off with old flames. And, if romance is what you're looking for there are many dating services and lots of places where you can post or read personal ads. You'll find adverts and links to these as soon as you start surfing the net.

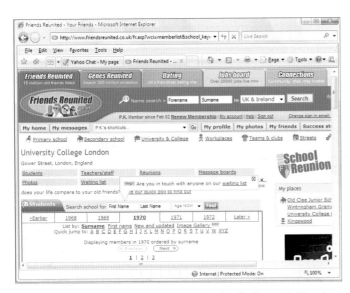

Friends Reunited is the UK's leading site for finding old friends and colleagues.

**Timesaver tip**

You can find Friends Reunited at www.friendsreunited.co.uk

**See also**

For more ways of meeting people, read about communities in Chapter 7.

# What can I download from the web?

What would you like? There's lots of stuff to download, some of it free, some of it at a price, and almost all of it easy to find and easy to handle.

## Music

Currently, the most popular type of download is music. New compression techniques allow CD-quality audio to be held in (relatively) small files, and the growth of high-speed, high-capacity broadband connections has made it practical to distribute music via the Internet. Apple's iPod player and its iTunes site have been responsible for much of the recent increase, but it really started with Napster and other 'file-sharing' sites, through which people allowed the music files on their own PCs to be downloaded across the Internet. This soon ran into copyright problems because recordings were being distributed without the artists' or recording companies' permission, and without paying for them. Compromises were reached, and now a small payment is required for most downloads. A lot is still available for free – and not just from new bands that are trying to make their name. In 2005, the BBC broke records when they offered Beethoven's symphonies for free download.

## Did you know?

Video will be the next big thing. There are already sites offering full length, DVD quality movies for downloading, or lower quality ones for online viewing. And it's not all pornography – there are sites like Movieflix that offer a good range of films for family viewing.

## See also

We will be looking at some of the Internet's downloadable resources in Chapter 4.

mp3.com is one of a number of sites offering free or low cost downloads of CD-quality recordings – and there is music here for all tastes. See for youself at www.mp3.com.

## Software

The Internet is the biggest software store in the world, and it's open all hours! There are millions of gigabytes worth of files out there, all ready to be downloaded.

The main source of files are the shareware sites. Much of the software on offer here is either free, or supplied with a request – not a requirement – for a small payment. Just because it is free or cheap, don't think this is not worth bothering with as some of it is very good indeed. You will also find files at the sites of computer software and hardware companies, who use the web to distribute new versions of their software or updates and 'patches' to fix the bugs in the programs they've already sold you.

## Other resources

As well as programs, the web is also a good source of other types of files, such as fonts, clip-art images, photos, and text files. You can even download books from the web, to read on-screen or to print for yourself – again, many of these are free, and the rest are cheaper than going to the bookshop.

Download.com is one of the leading shareware sites, with thousands of files – all checked for viruses – available for download.

**Important**  **2**

Windows has an Update facility that can be set to check Microsoft's site regularly for updates, and to download and install them, automatically or under your control. Once you start to go online, it is very important to keep your Windows system up to date. There are people who delight in finding the flaws in Windows software and writing viruses to exploit them. The updates help to protect your computer.

## What do I need to get online?

When I first went online, in the late 1980s, getting connected required relatively expensive equipment and quite a lot of technical know-how – and there wasn't that much to do once you were online. Today, the costs are minimal, no technical knowledge is needed, and the online possibilities are amazing.

To get connected you need four things:

- **A computer** – any reasonably modern computer will do. It does not need to be state-of-the-art or top-of-the-range. If you are buying a new system, the cheapest Windows Vista PC will do the job, or even a second-hand Windows XP machine – as long as it is in good condition. Apple Macs are fine, and less susceptible to viruses (which are mainly written by Windows programmers), but they are more expensive to buy and there is less software available for Apples. Cost: under £400 for a desktop PC complete with Windows, Internet Explorer, Windows Mail, a word processor, and other entry-level but adequate software. Spend more only if you need a higher specification machine, or more sophisticated software for other uses.

- **A modem** – the device which links the computer to the phone line. You need a different type of modem for a dial-up connection down a normal phone line than for a broadband connection. Modern PCs are usually sold with a standard modem built-in, and so are ready for a dial-up connection. If you take the broadband alternative, a suitable modem will be supplied as part of the deal.

- **A phone line** – or more to the point, a phone socket within reach of the computer. If necessary, you can get extension phone leads at any good DIY store. Cost: £5–£10.

- **An account with an Internet service provider** – the company that will link you to the internet and provide you with your email address and web space if you want to set up a site.

### Timesaver tip

If you regularly spend time away from home, think about a laptop instead of a desktop PC – entry-level machines are around £500. You may also need a pay-as-you-go dial-up account for when you are away from home.

There are basically three types of ISP account.

- A broadband connection gives high-speed access to the Internet. This uses the normal phone line, but the line has to be reconfigured at the exchange before it can be used. Not all local exchanges have this capacity, so the first thing to do is to check that broadband is available in your area. Broadband users can connect at the start of the day and leave it connected until they shut down – it costs nothing and causes no problems as the phone can be used for normal calls while the computer is online.

  There are several variables: speed, download limits, number of email addresses that you can run from one account, and whether or not you are given web space. The cost will vary to match, from around £15 to £30 a month. You only need the very high speeds and high download limits if you intend to download a lot of music or videos. All broadband ISPs offer a free modem, but you must sign up for a minimum of 1 year.

  Broadband providers include AOL, Orange, BTInternet, Virgin and most other phone companies.

- A monthly contract dial-up account. This will work on any phone line – you can even connect through a mobile if you have a suitable lead. Though far slower than broadband, dial-up is what we all managed with perfectly happily until recently. Expect to pay £15 a month, and to get unlimited access on an 0800 line.

- A pay-as-you-go dial-up account. These also run on the standard phone line. They typically cost 1p per minute, with the charging done through your phone bill as the connections are to 0844 or 0845 numbers. If you mainly use the Internet for email, with occasional dips into the web to look things up, then pay-as-you-go can be an economic solution – one brief phone call a day to collect and receive your email should add up to a little over £1 a month. Dial-up account providers include AOL, Orange and many smaller firms, including my own excellent TCP.

The problem is, you don't really know what you need until you have been active online for a while. So here's a suggestion. Several ISPs – notably AOL – offer a free month's trial of their dial-up service. Try it. See how you get on, and make an informed decision at the end of the month.

# How do I choose an ISP?

2

# Using Internet Explorer

## Introduction

Internet Explorer is the browser that is supplied as part of Windows. It is a powerful piece of software – easy to use but with all the sophisticated features that you need to get the best out of browsing the World Wide Web. In this chapter you will learn about the main features of Internet Explorer, and how to configure it to suit the way you work.

The screenshots are from Internet Explorer 7.0, the latest version at the time of writing. If you have an earlier version, go to Microsoft's web site at www.microsoft.com and download I.E.7.0 now – it is a better, safer system than the earlier ones.

The screenshots may not quite match your screen because your Windows Display Properties (the ones that control the colours, text styles and other aspects of the screen display) may be different.

### What you'll do

Discover the Internet Explorer window

Explore the standard toolbar

Use the Address bar

Use Auto Complete

Select and search for addresses

Use, add and organise favourites

Use and add feeds

Set feed properties

Use, view and search History

Create a shortcut to a site

Save a web page

Save a picture from a web page

View pictures in the Gallery

Save text from a web page

Use Print Preview and Page Setup

Print web pages and pictures

Browse and search for Help

Get Help on or offline

# Discovering the Internet Explorer window

We had a quick look at the Internet Explorer window in Chapter 1, but concentrated on the absolute essentials. Let's have a closer look at the display, and take in more of its features.

Toolbar handles          Title bar                                          Links toolbar

Explorer bar          Menu bar          Address toolbar          Standard toolbar

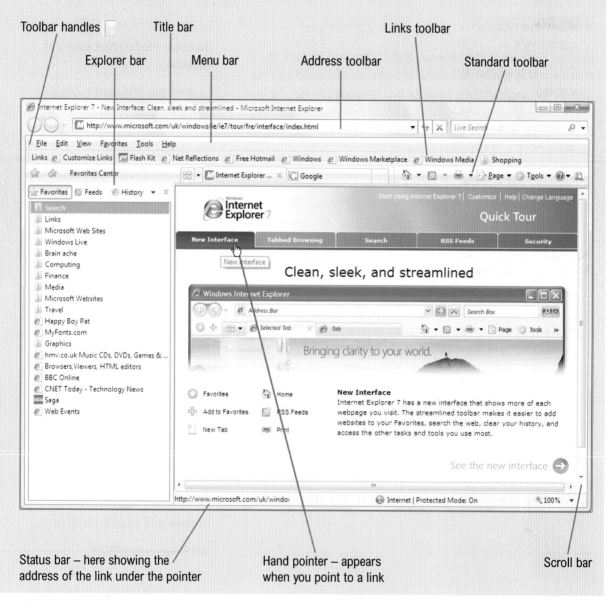

Status bar – here showing the address of the link under the pointer

Hand pointer – appears when you point to a link

Scroll bar

## The toolbars

■ **Title bar** – shows the title of the Web page, which is not the same as its URL.

■ **Menu bar** – gives you access to the full set of commands.

This and the Links bar can be hidden if not wanted.

■ **Standard toolbar** – with tools for the most commonly-used commands.

■ **Address bar** – shows the URL (Uniform Resource Locator, the address and filename) of the page. Addresses can be typed here.

■ **Links toolbar** – links to selected sites. There are predefined links to Microsoft's sites, but you can change these and add your own links.

■ **Toolbar handles** – you can drag these to move the toolbars.

## Other features

■ **Explorer bar** – can be opened when it is needed, to display your History (links to the places visited in the last few days) or your Favourites (links to selected pages), or to run a search for information. Clicking on a link in the Explorer bar will display its page in the main window.

■ **Divider** – click and drag on this to adjust the width of the Explorer bar. You may need more space when using the Explorer bar for a search.

■ **Scroll bars** – will appear on the right and at the bottom if a web page is too deep or too wide to fit into the window.

■ **Status bar** – shows the progress of incoming files for a page. When they have all downloaded, you'll see 'Done'. It also shows the address in a link when you point to it.

**See also**

Pages 76 to 78 for more on displaying and moving toolbars.
Page 43 for how to use the Address bar.

3

# Exploring the standard toolbar

## The navigation tools

Use these to move between the pages you have already visited during the session:

**1** Back takes you to the page you have just left.

**2** Forward reverses the Back movement.

**3** The drop-down page list allows you to select from the last dozen or so pages.

## The standard toolbar

These buttons contain almost all of the controls that you need when you are online.

**1** Home goes to your start page – your jumping off point into the web. This can be your own home page or any other page.

**2** Feeds are used to alert you to new content in web pages. Not all sites offer a feeds service – click the button when you are on a page to see if feeds are available from it.

**3** Print prints the current page (text and graphics).

**4** Page opens a menu. Its commands are related to the content of pages. Note these:

■ Copy copies text or images for pasting into a document.

■ Save As stores a copy of the page.

■ Send Page/Link by Email connects you to Windows Mail to send someone the page, or a link to it.

■ Zoom enlarges the text and graphics.

■ Text size enlarges, or reduces, the text size.

**5** Tools also leads to a menu. Its commands are more varied - key ones include:

■ Pop-up Blocker: turn this on to block pop-up windows – usually carrying adverts – opening when you visit web pages.

■ Phishing Filter should be turned on to restrict those emails that try to con you into giving out banking and other personal details.

■ Full screen removes the toolbars and uses the entire screen to display a page.

■ The Toolbars submenu controls the display of toolbars and sidebars.

■ Internet Options allow you to configure Explorer to suit your needs.

**6** Help opens a menu offering alternative ways to get help.

**7** Research opens the Research task pane.

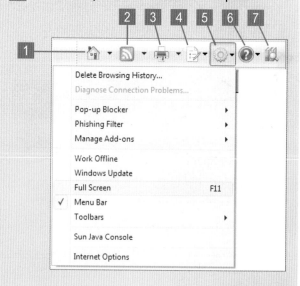

The Address bar serves two purposes. As you navigate round the Web, the address of the current page is shown in it, but you can also use the bar actively. If you type an address into it, the browser will then go to that page. And you rarely need to type an address twice! Internet Explorer remembers every address that goes into the Address bar – not just those that you enter, but also those that are generated by sites as you move around them. In practice, this means that to return to any site – or to a page within a site – you do not normally need to retype the URL.

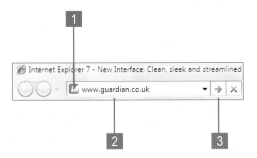

## Type an address

1. Click into the Address bar.
2. Type in the address, exactly as it was given to you.
3. Press [Enter] or click .

3

### Important !

Near enough is not good enough when typing web addresses. You must type them exactly. Watch the punctuation, especially the use of under_scores and full.stops.

# Using AutoComplete

When you start to type an address, Internet Explorer searches through past ones and offers those that start with the same letters, with the best guess being popped into the Address bar to complete the address. This is AutoComplete.

1 Start to type an address that you have typed before.

2 Accept the completed address in the Address bar or select it from the drop-down list.

3 Press [Enter] or click →.

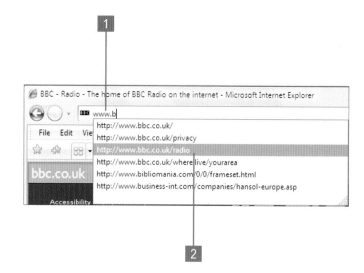

## Did you know?

AutoComplete is optional. It can be turned on and off through the Options – see page 95.

The addresses that you have typed – but not those generated within sites – are stored at hand in a list that drops down from the Address bar. You can select one from here by simply opening the list.

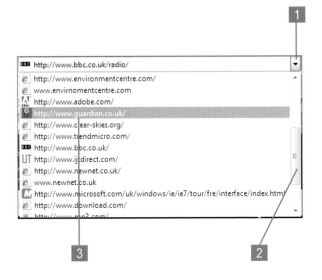

1. Click the down arrow on the right of the Address bar.
2. Scroll through the list to find the address.
3. Click on the one you want.

3

## Important

The addresses that you can recall into the Address bar are part of the History facility (see page 56). They are discarded when they reach their time limit. If you want to clear them immediately click Delete... in the Internet Options dialogue box, then click Delete history... in the Delete Browsing History options.

Delete Browsing History

**Temporary Internet Files**
Copies of webpages, images, and media that are saved for faster viewing.
Delete files...

**Cookies**
Files stored on your computer by websites to save preferences such as login information.
Delete cookies...

**History**
List of websites you have visited.
Delete history...

**Form data**
Saved information that you have typed into forms.
Delete forms...

**Passwords**
Passwords that are automatically filled in when you log on to a website you've previously visited.
Delete passwords...

About deleting browsing history          Delete all...          Close

## Searching for an address ▶

If you do not know the address of a website, you may still be able to find it – or rather, get Internet Explorer to find it for you. If you type the name of the organisation, or any other word that may identify the site into the Address bar, Internet Explorer will automatically pass it to the Live Search facility which will suggest possible sites.

1 Type a name or keyword that may identify the site you want.

2 Press [Enter] or click →.

3 Wait a moment while Internet Explorer connects to Live Search to run the search. A list of possible sites will be displayed.

4 Look through the list for the most likely link, then click on it to go to the site.

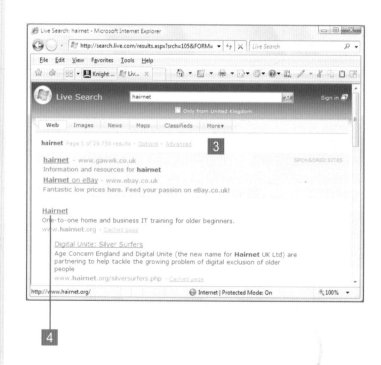

### ? Did you know?

You can search for lots more than just websites at Live Search. Go to www.live.com and explore.

A favourite is an address stored in an easily-managed list. To return to a favourite place, you simply click on it in the list.

Favourites can be accessed through the Favourites menu or through the Explorer bar. We'll start with the menu approach.

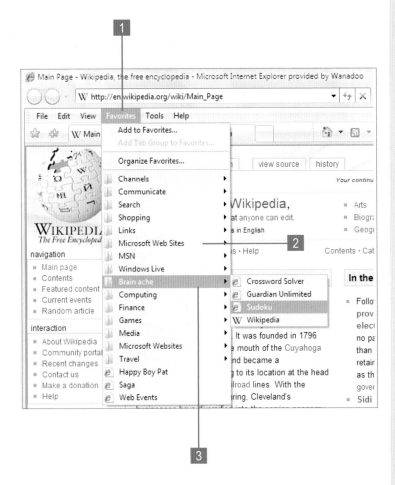

1 Open the Favourites menu.

2 If the Favourite is in a folder, open its sub-menu.

3 Click on the one you want.

3

### Did you know?

Even if you haven't yet added a Favourite of your own, there should be some already in the list – mainly to Microsoft's sites.

# Adding a favourite

Addresses are a pain to type. One mistake and either you don't get there at all, or you find yourself at a totally unexpected site. (Try www.microsfot.com sometime.) Favourites are one way of being able to return to a site without having to retype its address.

1 Find a good site!

2 Open the Favourites menu and click Add to Favourites…

3 The Add Favourites dialogue box will open. Internet Explorer will have derived the Name from the page. If you are happy with the name and want to add the link to the main Favourites list click Add.

otherwise

4 Edit the suggested name, or type a new one – you want something that will work well as a menu item, so aim for short but meaningful.

5 To store it in a folder click the bar to open the Create in list.

**6** In the enlarged dialogue box,
if there is a suitable folder,
click on it.

**7** If not click New Folder.

**8** Type a name for the folder
and click Create.

**9** Back at the Add Favourite
dialogue box click Add.

3

# Organising your favourites

You can store your favourites in one simple list, but this soon gets unwieldy. If there are more than about twenty items, the menu takes up too much screen space and it can be hard to find the favourite you want. The solution is to organise your favourites into folders, which then become sub-menus in the Favourites system. It's easy to create new folders and to move entries into them.

1. Click Organise Favourites on the Favourites menu

2. Click New Folder .

3. A new folder will appear. Give it a suitable name.

4. Drag the link on to the folder and drop it in. If you pause over the folder first, it will open and you can then place the link exactly where you want it in the list.

   or

5. Select the link and click Move... .

6. Select the folder from the list

7. Click OK .

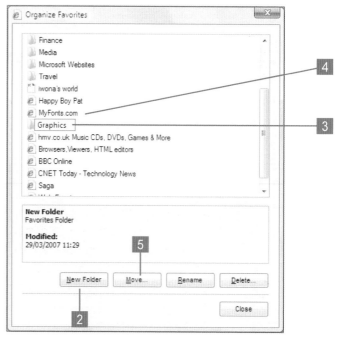

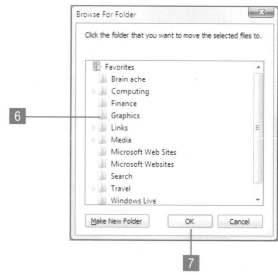

The Favourites can also be displayed in the Explorer Bar, and can be handled in two ways. You can either open the Favourites Centre temporarily to select a single site, or 'pin' the centre into place if you want to visit several favourites in the same session.

## Using Favourites in the Explorer bar

1 Click ☆ to open the Favorites Centre in the Explorer Bar.

2 Open folders as necessary and select the link. The Centre will automatically close as the linked site is opened in the main area.

or

3 Click ◄ to pin the Centre into place.

4 Click on the links to display the sites in the main pane.

5 Click ✕ to close the Centre when you have finished.

### Timesaver tip

To add the current page to your favourites while the Favourites Centre is open, click ✿ on its toolbar and select Add to Favourites... from the drop-down menu.

# Using feeds

Feeds are brief outlines, which are sent out by sites to subscribers to alert them to news stories or other new material. The feeds carry links to those stories.

Internet Explorer comes with subscriptions to three feeds – Microsoft at home, Microsoft at work and MSNBC News. Other feeds can be added easily. Most newspapers and broadcasters offer feed services – as do many bloggers.

**1** Click ☆ to open the Favourites Centre in the Explorer Bar.

**2** Click ⬛ Feeds to switch to the Feeds list.

**3** Click on a site name to display its feeds in the main window.

**4** Click on the headline or the Go arrow to go to the site to read the full article.

**5** You can normally sort feeds by date or title. In the Sort by area, click on Date or Title to sort into order – click again to reverse the order.

**6** Some sites offer a Filter by category option – click on the category you want to view.

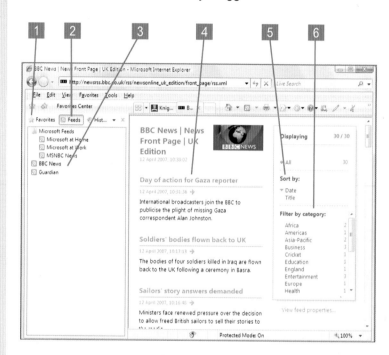

When you are on a site that offers a feed service, the  button in the command bar will turn orange, instead of its usual grey. Clicking on the button will start the process for subscribing to the default feed service. Sometimes, this is the only one; sometimes there are alternatives – which is why the best way to start is not by clicking directly on this button, but on its arrow to open the menu.

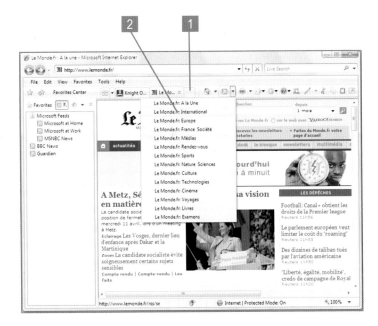

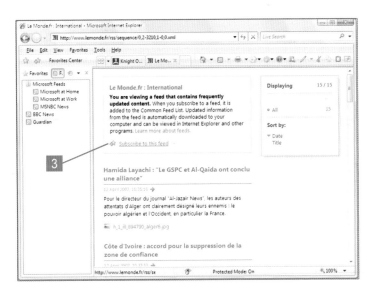

1 When you are at a site offering feeds, click on the arrow beside the Feeds icon.

2 If there are alternatives, select a feed. If not – click the single link.

3 At the subscription page, look for the Subscribe to this feed link – it will often be in a box at the top left.

3

# Adding feeds (cont.)

**4** At the dialogue box, edit the name as required.

**5** To add it to the main Feeds list, simply click [ Subscribe ].

or to store it in a folder

**6** Click [ New Folder ] to create a new folder.

**7** Enter a name and click [ Create ].

**8** Drop down the Create in list and select the folder.

**9** Click [ Subscribe ].

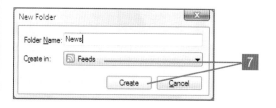

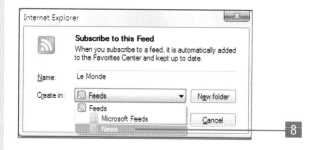

Internet Explorer will normally check each feed for new updates every day, and will store 200 items. You can change the update schedule and the number of items to store.

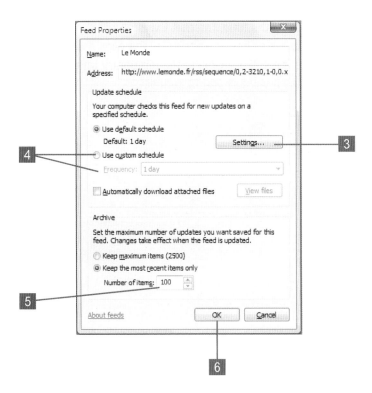

1 Open the Favorites Centre and display the feeds.

2 Right-click on the feed that you want to customise, and select Properties from the menu.

**To change the default schedule**

3 Click Settings and pick the frequency of updating – from every 15 minutes to once a week.

**To change the schedule for that feed only**

4 Select Use custom schedule, then pick the frequency from the drop-down list.

**To change the number of items to store**

5 Type a new value, or use the arrows to adjust the value in the Number of items list.

6 Click OK.

# Using History

As you browse, each page is recorded in the History list as an Internet shortcut – i.e. a link to the page. Clicking the History button opens the History list in the Explorer bar. Click a link from here to go to the page.

If you are online at the time, Internet Explorer will connect to the page. If you are offline, it will display the page if all the necessary files are still available in the temporary Internet files folder, otherwise it will ask you to connect.

1. Click on the History button in the Favourites Centre.

2. Click on the name to open the day and the site folders (if relevant in that view).

3. Click on a link.

4. To close a folder, click on its name.

5. Click ⊠ to close the Explorer bar when you have finished.

## See also

You can control how long pages are kept in the History, and how much space is set aside for temporary Internet files. See pages 80 and 81 to find out how to do this.

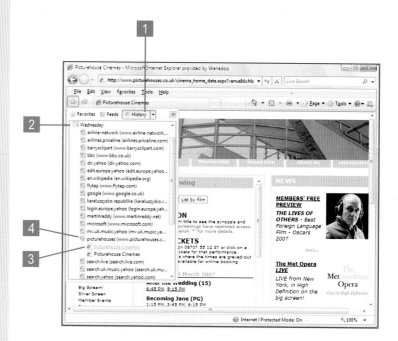

The History list can be viewed in four ways:

- **By Date** groups the links into folders by date and then by site. This is useful if you know when you were last there, but not the name of the site – and you may well not know where a page was if you reached it through a hyperlink.

- **By Site** groups the links into folders by site. This is probably the most convenient view most of the time.

- **By Most Visited** lists individual page links in the order that you visit them most. If there are search engines or directories that you regularly use as start points for browsing sessions, they will be up at the top of the list.

- **By Order Visited Today** lists the individual pages in simple time order. Use this view to backtrack past the links that are stored in the drop-down list of the Back button.

## Viewing the History list

1. In the Explorer bar, click the History ▾ button to display the options.

2. Select the view which you think will enable you to find the required page fastest.

3

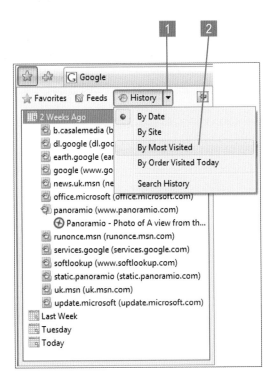

## Timesaver tip

If the History list starts to get clogged up, you can delete sites or individual pages within sites. Right-click on the site or page and select Delete from the pop-up menu that appears.

## Searching the History list

If you have been very active online in the last few days, the History list may have so many entries that it is difficult to find a page whichever view you use. When this happens, a search through the History list may be the answer.

1. In the Explorer bar, click the arrow on `History` and select Search History from the menu.

2. Type a word that will identify the page.

3. Click `Search Now` to start the search.

4. If there are any matching pages in the History list, they will be listed. Select one to go to the page.

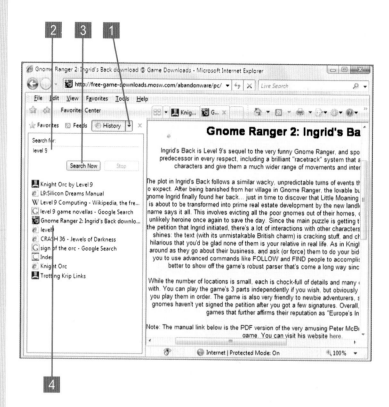

If you like, you can create a shortcut on the desktop to give you a quick route back to a special site. Use these sparingly! If you fill your desktop with shortcuts – and people do – it is really quite difficult to find the one you want.

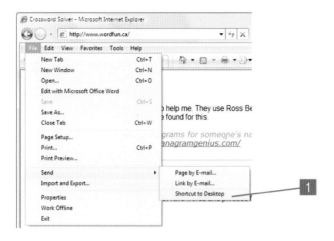

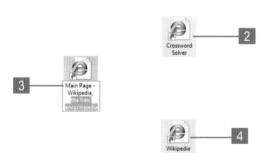

1 Open the File menu and point to Send, then select Shortcut to Desktop. Confirm at the prompt.

2 Look on the desktop. You should find a new shortcut at the bottom of the right-hand column.

3 If a page has a long name or identifier, the shortcut text may need editing. Click on the shortcut and press [F2].

4 Edit or retype the name so that it is short and meaningful.

5 When you want to return to the site, double-click the shortcut. If Internet Explorer is not open, it will start up, connect to the Internet and then head for the site.

## For your information

If the desktop is hidden beneath several application windows, you can minimize them all at a stroke by clicking the Show Desktop icon in the Quick Launch toolbar. Click it again if you want to restore the screen display.

Show Desktop

# Saving a web page

You sometimes find really interesting pages that you would like to have close at hand for future use – on and offline. Saving a page stores the files on your PC. And if you save it as a web page, complete, then all the files, including any images, sounds or videos will be saved.

1. Find a really interesting page!
2. Open the File menu and select Save As...
3. Select the folder that you want to save the file in. If necessary, click Browse Folders to open up the full box and select the folder there.
4. Edit the page name if necessary, so that it clearly identifies the page.
5. Set the Save As type to Web Page, complete.
6. Click [Save].

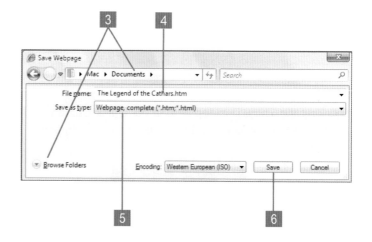

To read a saved web page you must open it with the File, Open command. Notice when you reach its folder that, as well as the page itself (marked with the extension .htm), there will normally also be a folder of the same name. The page's images and other files are stored here.

## Reading a saved page

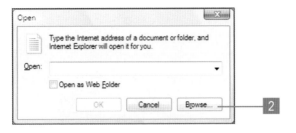

1 Open the File menu and select Open...

2 At the Open dialogue box, click Browse... .

3 At the Internet Explorer dialogue box, locate the folder, where the file is stored.

4 Select the file from the display.

5 Click Open .

3

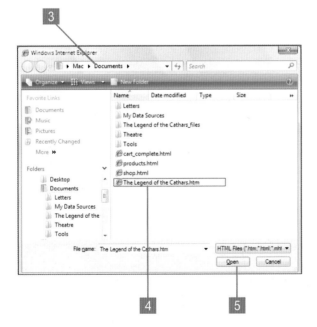

## Saving a picture from a web page

If you come across a picture in a web page that you would like to keep for future viewing, it can easily be saved to a disk.

But do note that all images on web pages are the copyright of the page's owner, and may not be used commercially without permission. This screenshot is from the Web Museum – an essential resource for art lovers. Find it at www.ibiblio.org/wm.

1 Point to the picture.

2 Right-click on the image and select Save Picture As... from the menu.

3 Select the Save in folder. Click Browse Folders to open the full dialogue box if necessary.

4 Edit the name or type a new one.

5 Click Save .

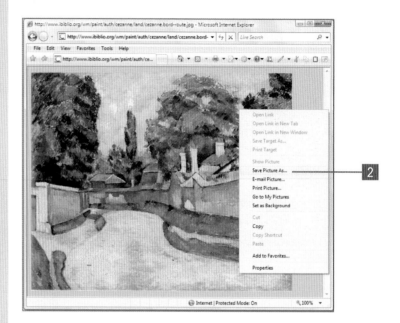

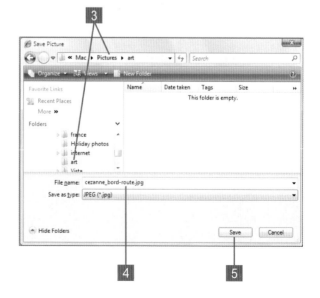

You can take images from web pages directly into Windows Photo Gallery, where you can edit, print, or add captions and tags, and file them as you would your own digital photos. If you normally use the Photo Gallery for your work with images, this may be the best way to handle images from the Web.

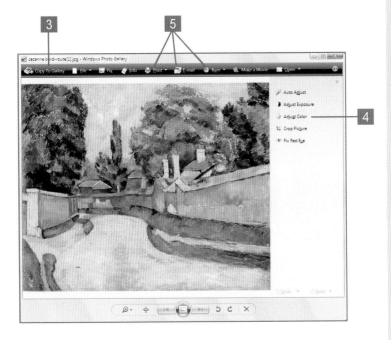

## Viewing pictures in the Gallery

1 Find an image you want to keep.

2 Open the File menu and select Edit with Windows Photo Gallery.

3 Click the Copy to Gallery button if you want to save a copy on your system.

4 Use the exposure, colour and crop controls if you want to edit the picture.

5 Print, email or burn to CD from the Gallery if you like.

## Important

Unless it explicitly says so, all the images that you find on the Web are copyright protected. You cannot use these images for profit, or republish them in any way, without the permission of the copyright owner.

# Saving text from a web page

There are two ways to save the text from a web page. You can save the page as a text file, but this may not be very successful. There are several ways of producing web pages, and with some of these, the Save routine will not save the visible text.

A second – and more reliable – method is to copy the text, paste it into a word processor and save it from there.

1. Highlight the text that you want to save.

2. Right-click on the highlighted area and select Copy from the menu.

3. Start your word processor.

4. Use Edit, Paste to copy the text.

5. Save the file as normal.

## Did you know?

There's a handy summary of the rules on copyright at www.is4profit.com – head for the business advice pages and follow the links to Business Law and Intellectual Property.

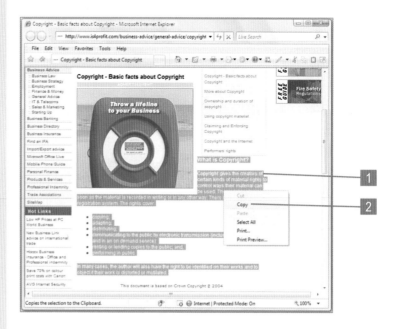

A sheet of A4 paper and a computer screen are rather different shapes, and pages can be laid out on the screen in different ways. What this means is that you can never be entirely sure what a web page will look like when it is printed, or how many sheets it will be printed on – unless you use Print Preview. If the preview is acceptable, you can send it straight to the printer; if adjusting the layout might give a better printout, you can open the Page Setup dialogue box and change the settings.

## Using Print Preview

1. Open the File menu and select Print Preview...

2. Use the arrows to work through the pages.

3. Set the Zoom level to look at details or the overall layout.

4. If you want to adjust the page layout, click ⚙ the Page Setup button (see the next page for more on this).

5. To print the page(s), click 🖶.

6. To return to the normal web page display without printing, click ❌.

### Timesaver tip

You can sometimes get better results by copying part or all of a page into your word processor and printing it from there.

# Adjusting the Page Setup

The Page Setup controls how pages fit onto paper. The key features are the orientation, and the margins. The headers and footers can include plain text or details of the web pages – Internet Explorer automatically adds codes to display the page's title, address, page numbers and date. You can move or remove these, or add your own text.

1. If you are in Print Preview, click ⊙ the Page Setup button.

   otherwise

2. Open the File menu and select Page Setup...

3. Check the Paper Size – it may be set to Letter and you probably use A4.

4. If a web page is too wide to fit on a normal sheet, change the Orientation to Landscape, so that it prints sideways.

5. To change the margin widths, click into the fields and type new values.

6. Edit the header and/or footer if required.

7. Click OK.

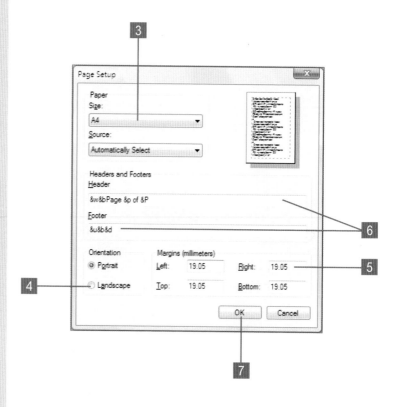

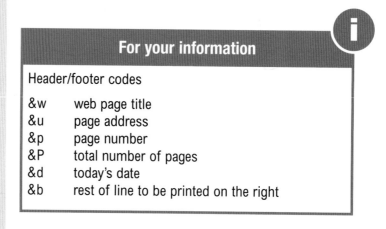

## For your information

Header/footer codes

| Code | Description |
| --- | --- |
| &w | web page title |
| &u | page address |
| &p | page number |
| &P | total number of pages |
| &d | today's date |
| &b | rest of line to be printed on the right |

If you just want a printed copy of the whole of the current page, you simply click the Print button. Sometimes you need to control the printout – you may only want part of a long page or a section of a framed page, or you may want to print sideways on the paper (landscape orientation), or print several copies. In these cases, you need to go into the Print dialogue box.

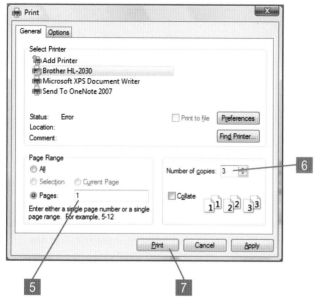

## Printing web pages

1 To print the current page, just as it is, click  ▾.

2 If you only want to print part of a page, use the mouse to select it now – you may sometimes find that additional items get selected alongside the part that you wanted. That's just the way web pages are!

3 If the page is very long, open the File menu and select Print Preview, to see which printed pages you will want.

4 Open the File menu and select Print.

5 Select the pages, if relevant.

6 Set the number of copies.

7 Click [ Print ].

3

# Printing framed pages

A framed page is divided into two or more parts, each of which can be changed separately. Typically there will be a frame across the top of the screen displaying the site's name and perhaps some advertising; a 'navigation' frame on the left side with links to the contents pages; and a larger frame, filling the rest of the window, where the content is displayed. You may well only want to print the content – this can be arranged.

**1** If you only want to print the contents of one frame, click into it now to select it.

**2** Open the File menu and select Print.

**3** At the Print dialogue box, click the Options label to switch to that tab.

**4** In the Print frames area, select what you want to be printed.

**5** If you want to print all linked documents, or a table of links, turn these options on.

**6** Switch to the General tab if you need to set other options.

**7** Click Print .

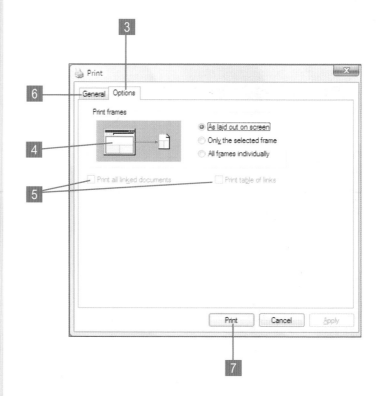

## For your information

The linked documents and table of links options are mainly of interest to web page developers, as it helps them to clarify the structure of a set of framed pages.

You can print a picture from a web page in a couple of clicks. But do note that this does not work well with larger pictures. If you try to print a large picture directly from Internet Explorer, you may well only get the left half of it – as much as can fit onto one sheet of paper. With bigger pictures you will get a better result if you save them, then open them in a graphics program, or insert them into a Word document and print from there.

## Printing a picture on a web page

1 Find a picure worth printing!

2 Right-click on the image and select Print Picture ... from the menu.

3 At the Print dialogue box, set any options as required and click Print .

3

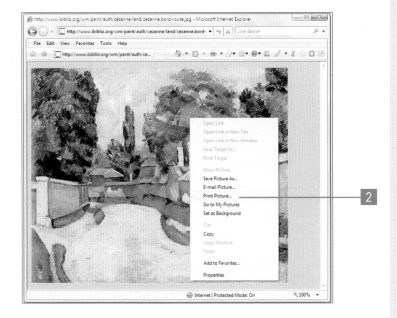

## Timesaver tip

Images that are too large for the window are automatically scaled down to fit, and the pointer becomes a magnifying glass. Click to switch the picture between full size (but only partly visible) and scaled to fit. And note the ⊕ 125% ▼ button at the bottom right. Click on the button to cycle between different zoom levels, or click on the arrow to open the menu and select a level.

# Browsing Help

Internet Explorer's Help system is not actually very helpful to the new user as it is rather light on the basics. It comes into its own once you have got past the initial stages and want to understand more advanced topics.

The pages can be accessed through the Browse or Search routines.

1. Open the Help menu and select Contents and Index to display the Help window.

2. Click on the Browse help button.

3. Click on a folder icon ▣ to open its set of Help pages.

4. Click on a topic icon ▣ to display it.

Home    Print    Browse    Ask

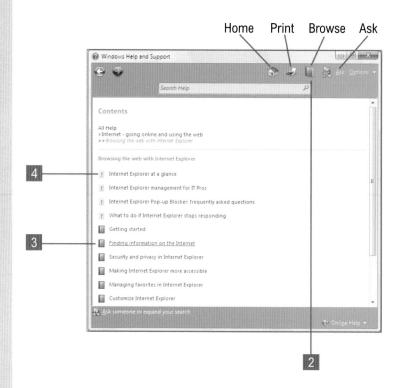

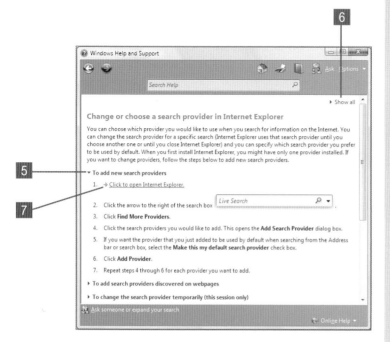

Windows Help and Support

Search Help

▶ Show all

**Change or choose a search provider in Internet Explorer**

You can choose which provider you would like to use when you search for information on the Internet. You can change the search provider for a specific search (Internet Explorer uses that search provider until you choose another one or until you close Internet Explorer) and you can specify which search provider you prefer to be used by default. When you first install Internet Explorer, you might have only one provider installed. If you want to change providers, follow the steps below to add new search providers.

▾ To add new search providers

1. → Click to open Internet Explorer.

2. Click the arrow to the right of the search box   Live Search   ✕ ▼ .

3. Click **Find More Providers.**

4. Click the search providers you would like to add. This opens the **Add Search Provider** dialog box.

5. If you want the provider that you just added to be used by default when searching from the Address bar or search box, select the **Make this my default search provider** check box.

6. Click **Add Provider.**

7. Repeat steps 4 through 6 for each provider you want to add.

▶ To add search providers discovered on webpages

▶ To change the search provider temporarily (this session only)

Ask someone or expand your search

Online Help ▼

**5** ▶ by a heading indicates that more information is available. Click on it to display the extra text.

**6** Click the Show all link to display the extra text under all of the headings.

**7** The → arrow beside a link indicates a task – typically opening Internet Explorer – that you must do before you can work through the rest of that Help item.

3

# Browsing Help (cont.)

## To use breadcrumbs

1. If you are not on a contents page (one with topic and folder headings) click the Back button to go back to the contents.

2. Click a link at the top of the page to step straight back to an earlier point in your travels through the contents.

## To read definitions

3. Click on the term – the text must be green – to open a pop-up panel containing a definition or explanation.

4. Click anywhere else on the page to close the pop-up when you have finished.

**Timesaver tip**

You can use the Back and Forward buttons to switch quickly between recently visited pages.

There's more to these Help pages than immediately meets the eye. Explore them, looking in particular for different coloured text, and links around the page. Don't miss these:

- You can always use the Back button to go back to the previous page, but while you are in the contents area – i.e. not on a topic page – there are 'breadcrumb' links at the top. These can take you back several steps at a time.

- If a word is in green, you can click on it to get an explanation or definition.

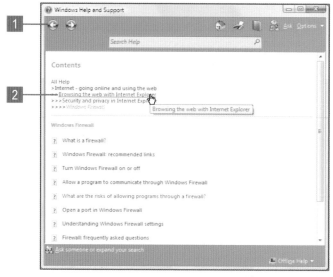

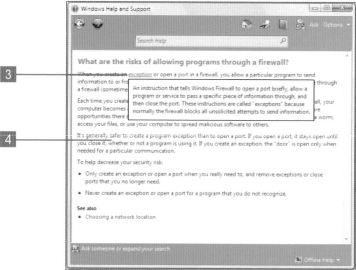

The Search slot offers you another way to get specific help. When you are asked for a 'keyword', this is not any kind of special word, but simply one which describes what you are looking for.

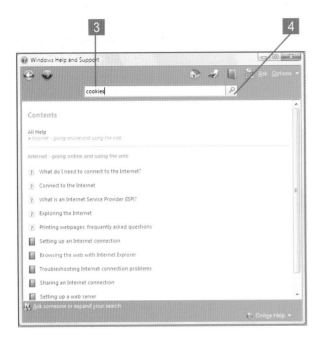

1 If the Help window is not present, open the Help menu and select Contents and Index to display it.

2 Click into the Search field.

3 Type a keyword.

4 Click 🔍 .

5 Click on a topic to select it.

6 Click ▭ to minimise or ✕ to close the Help window when you have finished.

3

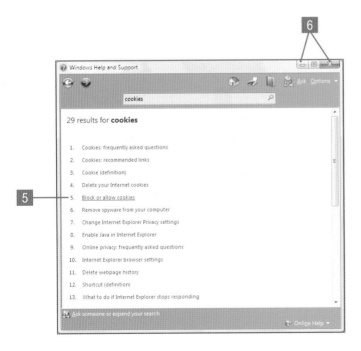

# Getting Help on and offline

When you search for help, the system normally searches not only the Help system on your PC but also the main Help database at Microsoft. Obviously, this is going to give you access to the latest and most comprehensive Help that is available. However, there may be times when you do not want to go online – especially if you have a slow dial-up connection – so here's how to control it.

## To stop using online Help

1 Click the Online Help button.

2 Select Get offline Help. The button will now say 'Offline Help'.

## To restore online Help

3 Click the Offline Help button.

4 Select Get online Help.

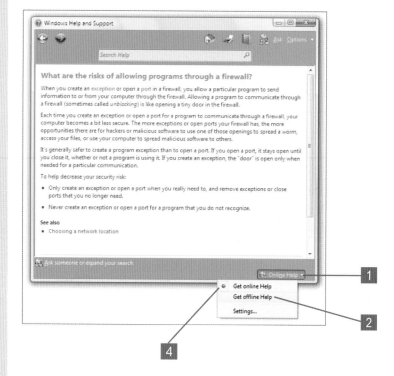

## Timesaver tip

If you want to change the default for online/offline Help, click the Settings option to open a dialogue box and turn the Include Windows Help and Support option on or off as required.

# Customising Internet Explorer

## Introduction

You can customise many aspects of Internet Explorer, from the cosmetic, such as the layout of the screen and the way it displays web pages, to the far more fundamental, including controlling what types of material, and from which sorts of sites it can be viewed.

Most of the customising is managed through the Internet Options, a multi-tab dialogue box. There are many options, and they should all be left at their default settings until you have spent enough time online to understand what they are about. For some of them, a couple of sessions will be enough for you to know what you want, but others should not be tackled lightly. In particular, you shouldn't touch anything that might reduce the security of your system until you are clear about the implications.

## What you'll do

**Change the toolbar layout**

**Lock the toolbars**

**Customise the Command Bar**

**Set the Home page**

**Manage temporary Internet files**

**Control the History**

**Set the web page colours, fonts and text size**

**Use the Security options**

**Learn about cookies**

**Change the Privacy settings**

**Block or allow pop-ups**

**Use Content Advisor**

**Add a rating system**

**Configure AutoComplete**

**Configure the Connections**

**Set the Advanced options**

**Manage and install add-ons**

**Get Adobe Reader**

**Use a linked application**

## Changing the toolbar layout

The three toolbars – and the menu bar – can be arranged in any order at the top of the window. Two or more bars can share a line, if you like. It's your browser – arrange the display to suit you.

Open the View menu and point to Toolbars to open the sub-menu.

Click Menu Bar or Links. These are toggle switches – click on the menu item to turn the bar on (✓) or off.

Click on the handle – the dotted line at the left end of the bar – of the toolbar you want to move.

Drag the toolbar up, down, left or right as required to put it into position, then release the handle.

If the toolbar is too long to fit into its space, it will have a » button at the end. Click on this to open a menu with the missing commands.

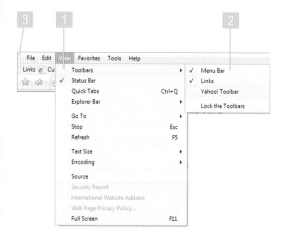

Once you have got the toolbars laid out as you want them, you can lock them into position so that they cannot be accidentally moved or hidden.

When toolbars are locked, their handles are removed, which will very slightly change the layout.

## Locking the toolbars

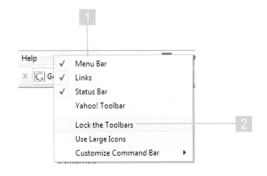

### Lock the toolbars

1 Right-click on any toolbar.

2 Select Lock the Toolbars from the pop-up menu.

### Unlock the toolbars

3 Right-click on any toolbar.

4 Click Lock the Toolbars again to remove the tick.

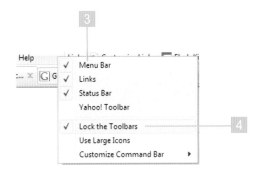

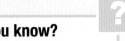

**Did you know?**

The Status bar can also be turned off to increase the main display area. Open the View menu and click Status bar to turn it on or off.

## Customising the Command Bar

The contents and appearance of the Command Bar can be altered to suit yourself. You can add or remove buttons, set the size of the icons and choose whether to show text labels on all buttons, on a selected few, or on none.

1 Right-click on any toolbar, point to Customise Command Bar and select Add or Remove commands.

2 To add a button, select it from the left-hand pane and click Add ->. It will be added above (i.e. to the left of) the selected item in the current list.

3 To change a button's position, use the Move Up and Move Down buttons.

4 To remove a button, select it and click Remove.

5 Click Close when you have finished.

6 Right-click on a toolbar, point to Customise Command Bar and click on Show All Text Labels, Selective Text or Icons only as required.

7 Right-click on a toolbar and click on Use Large Icons to toggle between large and small icons.

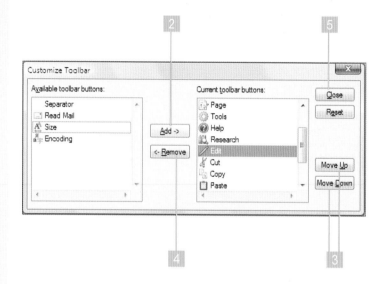

### Timesaver tip

You can hide or display text labels from the Customise Command Bar menu.

### Did you know?

If you make a mess of the display – it can happen all too easily! – click Reset to restore the default selection.

The term 'home page' has two meanings. It can refer to the top page at a website, but it also refers to the page that the browser connects to when you first go online (or when you click the Home button). Some people like to start their online sessions at one place – typically a site where they can get the latest news, weather or share prices, and which has a directory or search engine that they can use to track down information, or a chat room where they regularly meet old (and new) friends. The default is either at MSN (MicroSoft Network) or at your Internet service provider's site. You can change it, any time you like.

## Setting the Home page

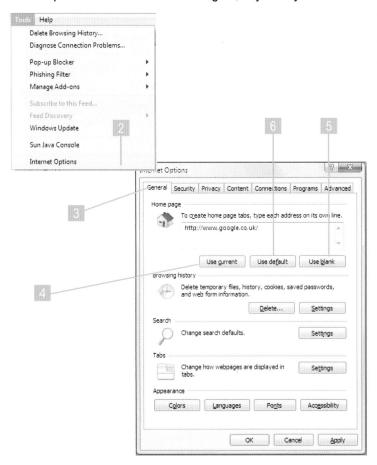

1 If there is a site that you want to use as your home page, go to it now.

2 Open the Tools menu and select Internet Options…

3 The dialogue box will open with the General tab on top. The Home Page is the first option.

4 To set the current page as the home page, click Use current .

5 If you start at different sites each time you go online, there is no point in wasting time going to a home page. Click Use blank .

6 If you want to revert to the default page, click Use default .

4

# Managing temporary Internet files

When you visit a web page, the files that create it are downloaded onto your PC. These files are retained, and if you return to that page, either during the same session or later, it will then use the stored files, which is quicker than downloading them again. It also means that you can revisit pages offline.

You can set the amount of storage space to suit the way you surf and the size of your hard disk. If you have plenty of space and you tend to go back to sites a lot – perhaps following up a succession of links from one start point, or perhaps because you like to revisit sites offline – give yourself a big cache. If space is a problem, cut the cache right down. And if you need to free up the disk space, delete all the stored files.

You can also choose when Internet Explorer should check for newer versions of the stored pages. The 'Automatically' setting should do the job – this will check at the first visit in a session, but select the 'Every visit to the page' option if your favourite sites are fast-changing ones, e.g. news sites.

1. Use Tools, Internet Options... to open the dialogue box.

2. If you need to clear space on your disk quickly, click Delete... then select the types of files to delete.

3. In the Browsing history area, click Settings .

4. Choose when to check for newer versions of stored pages.

5. Click the arrows, or edit the numbers to set the amount of disk space.

6. Click OK .

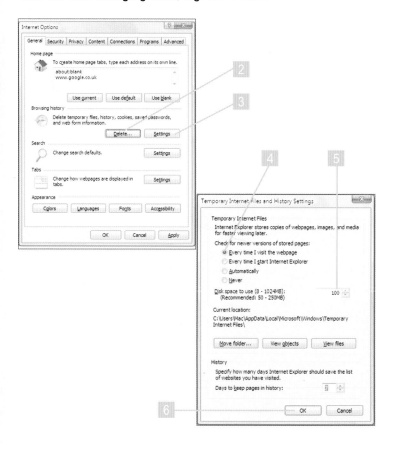

If you visit a lot of sites during your online sessions, and/or have set the number of days to keep the History links to a high value, then your History list could get very long. Beyond a certain point, its value as an aid to better browsing starts to diminish. You are probably best to set the days to no more than seven. The situations in which the History is most useful are those where you want to look back in leisurely offline time at pages that you glanced at while online, and you are most likely to do that either on the same day or within a couple of days. When you find sites that you will want to return to regularly, don't use the History – add them to your Favourites.

## Controlling the History

1. Use Tools, Internet Options… to open the Internet Options dialogue box. Click Settings.

2. Type a new value or use the arrows to adjust the number of days.

3. Click OK to save the change and exit.

4. Click Apply to save without closing the dialogue box.

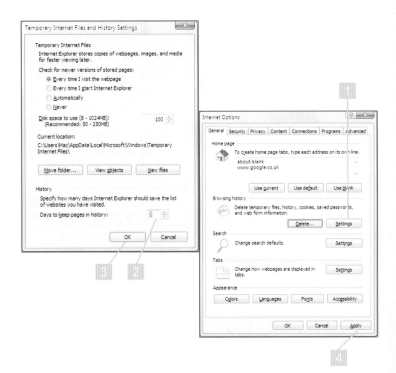

# Setting the web page colours

When people are creating web pages, they can choose what colours to use for the background, the main text, and the text that carries a hyperlink – when it is unvisited, visited or when the mouse is hovering over it. But page builders don't always bother to set the colours, and the Window's default colours will be used. You can change these.

You can also insist that your own choices are used even where they have been set by the page builder, and you may want to do this in the interests of visibility. (Some people have very strange ideas of what makes a good-looking page!)

1 Use Tools, Internet Options... to open the Internet Options dialogue box.

2 Click ⬚ Colors ⬚.

3 Clear the checkbox by Use Windows colours.

4 At the Colours dialogue box, click on a colour that you want to change.

5 Select a new colour from the palette and click ⬚ OK ⬚.

6 Click ⬚ OK ⬚ again at the Colours dialogue box.

This will set the colours where the page's creator has not specified them. To force the use of your colour scheme, carry on...

7 Click ⬚ Accessibility ⬚.

8 Tick the Ignore colours... checkbox.

9 Click ⬚ OK ⬚.

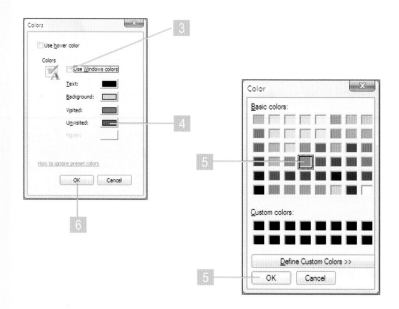

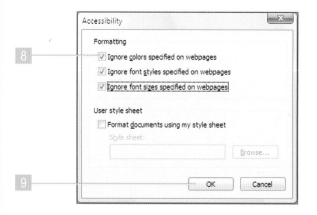

Web page builders can also set the fonts to be used on a page. This is done far less often than setting colours. The problem is this. To be sure that the specified font will be there, you must download it, along with the page and that slows things down.

There are two fonts: the web page font is used for virtually all the text, including headings and captions; the plain text font is used where the page builder has deliberately left the text unformatted for a special effect.

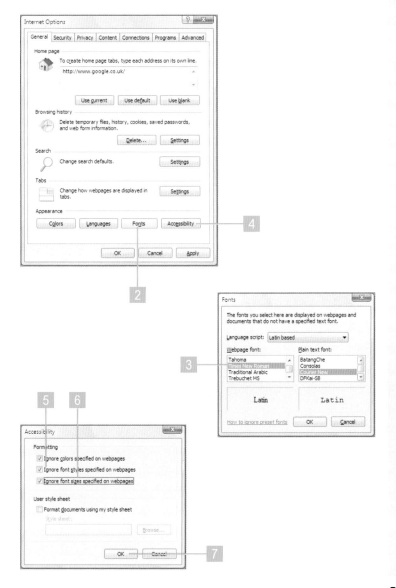

## Setting the web page fonts

1. Use Tools, Internet Options... to open the Internet Options dialogue box.

2. Click `Fonts`.

3. Pick fonts for the web page and for plain text. This will set the fonts where they are not specified.

4. To insist on their use, click `Accessibility`.

5. Tick the Ignore font styles specified on web pages checkbox.

6. To fix the text size, tick the Ignore font sizes specified on web pages checkbox.

7. Click `OK`.

# Setting the text size

Only the font names can be set in the Internet Options dialogue box. If you want to set the font size, you do it from the View menu or Text Size button. This makes setting the size quicker and simpler, which it needs to be as you may want to increase the text size for one site, but reduce it again on another. People have different ideas about what makes a page good to look at and easy to read!

The size change is applied to the different levels of headings as well as to the main text, with everything being made proportionately larger or smaller.

1 At any point while viewing a web page, open the View menu and point to Text Size.

2 Pick a text size.

or

3 Open the Page menu on the command bar and point to Text Size.

4 Pick a new size from the Largest to Smallest list.

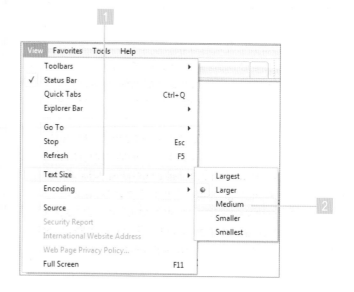

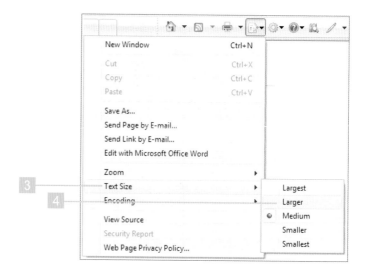

There would be fewer security problems if all web pages were simply displays of text and images, but some are more than this. They can contain active and interactive elements, which make pages more interesting and responsive, but also let malicious people create problems for others. These elements are small programs written in languages such as Java and ActiveX. They may be merely decorative or an essential part of the page's functionality – Java is often used to create pop-up menus for navigating around a site, while ActiveX controls are regularly used by online banks and retailers to create secure connections.

The options on the Security tab let you control whether, and in what circumstances, these programs are allowed to run. If you disable them, you will find that you cannot use some useful and perfectly safe sites. If you allow them to run on any page, there is a danger that one day you will find that a program has got into your PC and erased files, or otherwise messed with the system.

The default settings give a sensible balance between security and usability, setting different levels of restrictions depending upon whether a page is on the internet in general, a local intranet (a web open only to people inside the organisation), a Trusted site or a Restricted site. For each zone, you can accept the default settings or set your own levels. To start with, check that default settings are in place – we will tweak these next.

# Checking the Security options

1. Use Tools, Internet Options... to open the Internet Options dialogue box.

2. Switch to the Security tab.

3. Select the Internet zone. It should be set to Medium-high. If no, click Reset all zones to default level .

4. If you work in an organisation with a local intranet, check that its level is set to Medium-low.

5. Initially there won't be any Trusted or Restricted sites.

6. Click OK or Apply .

See also

Adding sites to Security zones is covered on the next page.

# Adding sites to Security zones

The Trusted and Restricted zones are lists of sites. Initially these lists are empty – it's up to you to add sites to them, though you may never feel the need.

A site should be added to the Trusted zone if it has active content that cannot run under the standard Internet zone security level – you will be told if this is the case – and which is owned by an organisation that you trust implicitly, e.g. your bank.

A site should be added to the Restricted zone if you want to be able to go to it, but are not convinced that the standard Internet zone level is sufficiently secure.

1. Use Tools, Internet Options... to open the Internet Options dialogue box.

2. Switch to the Security tab.

3. Select the Trusted or Restricted zone.

4. Click ___Sites___.

5. Type the address.

6. Click ___Add___.

7. To remove a site from the list, select it and click ___Remove___.

8. Click ___OK___.

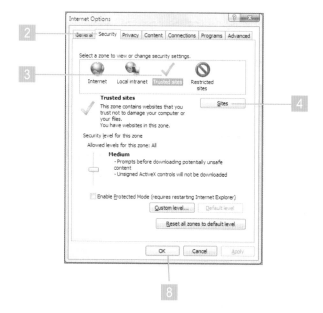

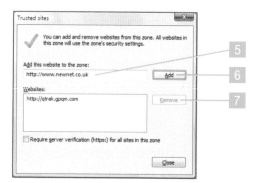

At the custom level, you can determine how Internet Explorer should respond to each type of active content. There are two or three options for each type:

- **Disable** will prevent that type of content from running on the browser.
- **Enable** turns the setting on, and permits the activity.
- **Prompt** will make the browser check with you before running the active content. This option is not always available.

To increase the security level – and to learn more about types of active content – switch to Prompt. Whenever the browser comes across a possible security problem, you will be alerted and have to OK it if you want the content to run. You will soon see which types of content occur most often. If it's clear that they are doing no harm, go back and Enable them.

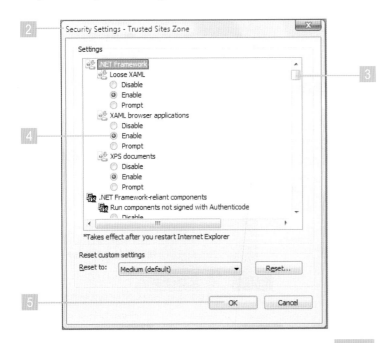

1 Use Tools, Internet Options… to open the Internet Options dialogue box and switch to the Security tab.

2 Select the Internet zone and click Custom level... to open the Security Settings dialogue box.

3 Scroll through the list of content types.

4 If you are very security conscious and don't mind being shut out from some sites, select 'Disable' for each one. If you like to know what's happening to your PC and are prepared to respond to every form of active content, select 'Prompt'. If you think I'm just paranoid and you want easy browsing, select 'Enable'.

5 Click OK .

## Important

The Custom settings are probably best left until you have more experience of the web and of different types of active content.

# What are cookies?

Cookies are small files that a website stores on your computer's hard disk, and which can be read by that site. Some sites use them to offers a 'personalised page' service – one where you can choose which features to display, or where the news or weather is tailored to your area – and here the cookie will hold the options and other details that you set. Some sites use cookies to keep track of their visitors, recording when they visited and which pages they viewed. Some go further and use cookies to build a database of their visitors' habits and preferences, and may sell this information on to other firms; on the other hand there are others which take great care not to misuse any personal data from cookies.

## Important !

You can choose whether or not to accept cookies, and what sort to accept.

First party cookies are those set by the website itself.

Third party cookies are those set by advertisers, or other linked sites, inside the page you are visiting.

Session cookies are only stored for the session and are deleted when Internet Explorer is shut down.

At the BBC site, a cookie can store your physical location so that you can get local weather forecasts whenever you go to that page.

Internet Explorer offers several levels of protection from cookies, but you can also control cookies yourself. They can be disabled, but this can create problems. It's not just that it may stop you from having personalised pages, there are some sites that you cannot use at all if you have disabled cookies. If you are suspicious of cookies, you can ask for a prompt before a cookie is set. This way you at least know who is writing to your hard disk, and can choose not to accept cookies from a site, but there are some irritating sites that want to write cookies for every new page – sometimes for every image – that you download.

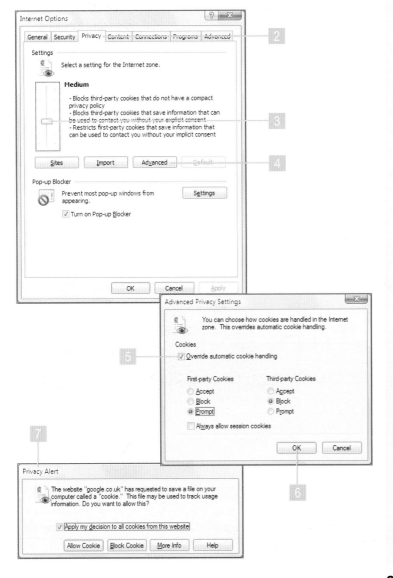

# Changing the Privacy settings

Use Tools, Internet Options… to open the Internet Options dialogue box.

Switch to the Privacy tab.

Move the slider to set the privacy level.

To fine-tune your cookie-handling, click Advanced .

At the Advanced Privacy Setting dialogue box, tick the Override automatic cookie handling checkbox then select how First and Third party cookies are to betreated.

Click OK .

If you opt for Prompts, you will get a Privacy Alert at every cookie-writing site. Respond as you see fit.

## Timesaver tip

If there are particular sites that you want to block or allow, click Sites and enter the site details at the dialogue box.

# Blocking pop-ups

▶

Pop-ups are windows that open on top of the Internet Explorer display. They usually have no menu bar, toolbar or other controls, and are typically quite small. Pop-ups are often used to carry adverts, and can be quite irritating, which is why Internet Explorer allows you to block pop-ups. They are also used quite legitimately to provide additional information or services off the main page – which is why Internet Explorer lets you allow pop-ups past the block.

1 Use Tools, Internet Options… to open the Internet Options dialogue box.

2 Switch to the Privacy tab.

3 Turn on Pop-up blocker.

4 Click Settings.

5 At the Pop-up Blocker Settings dialogue box, tick the Play a sound… option if you want to be alerted when a pop-up is blocked.

6 If you want to be able to allow pop-ups selectively, tick the Show Information Bar… option.

7 Set the Filter Level to High. If you find that this blocks too much, then return to here and set it to Medium.

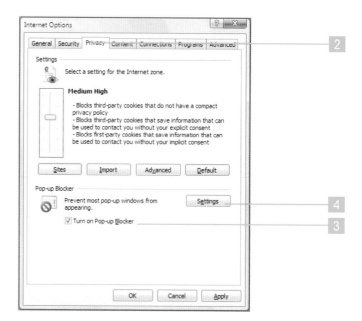

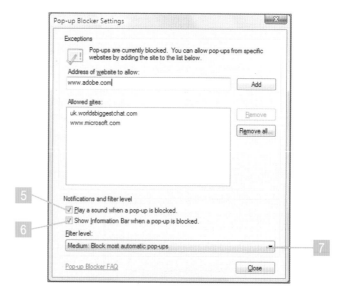

You may find, especially if the pop-up filter level is set to high, that you cannot use some pages properly – you click on a link and nothing happens (apart from the pop-up blocked sound). If the Information Bar is open, you can allow the pop-ups – either for just the current page or for the site every time you visit. You can also add sites to a list of exceptions so that their pop-ups are always allowed.

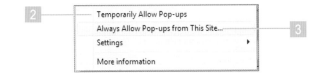

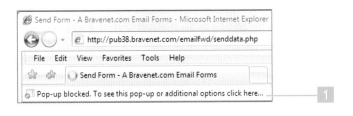

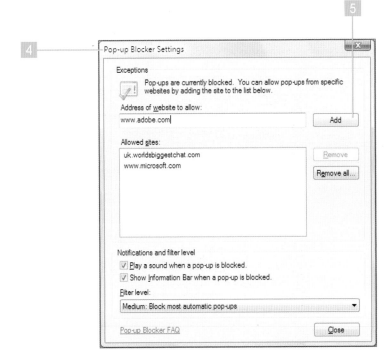

## Allowing pop-ups

When a pop-up is blocked and the Information Bar appears, click on the bar.

To allow the pop-up to be opened from the current page, select Temporarily Allow Pop-ups.

or

Select Always Allow Pop-ups from This Site… to add the site to the list of exceptions.

To add a site directly to the pop-ups allowed list, go to the Privacy tab of the Internet Options dialogue box and click Settings to open the Pop-up Blocker Settings dialogue box.

Type the address of the website and click Add.

# Using Content Advisor

If children can use your PC to access the Internet you may want to use Content Advisor to limit the sites that they can visit. This works through a system of ratings, and initially uses those set by ICRA – Internet Content Rating Association, which rate sites on language, nudity, sex and violence. You can set what level of each of these is acceptable and only sites within those limits will then be accessible.

There is a problem though – the system is voluntary and many perfectly safe sites do not have an ICRA rating. If a site is unrated, you can either allow free access or control access through a password.

## Set Content options

1. Use Tools, Internet Options... to open the Internet Options dialogue box.

2. Switch to the Content tab.

3. If you want to control how a child or grandchild uses the computer, click [Parental Controls] and turn on the Parental Controls for that user.

4. In the ContentAdvisor area, click [Enable...].

5. On the Ratings tab, select each category in turn and adjust the slider to set the limits – as you move the slider the description will change to show what is permitted.

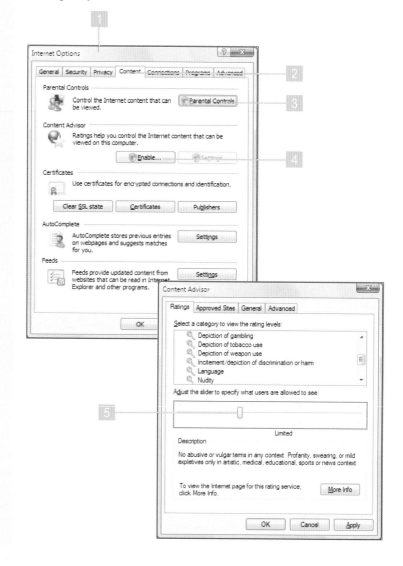

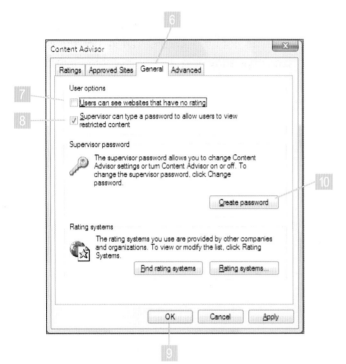

6 Switch to the General tab and look at the User options area.

7 If you want to allow access to unrated sites, tick the checkbox.

8 If you want to allow access to unrated or restricted sites for those who know the password, tick the checkbox.

9 Click [ OK ].

10 The first time that you use Content Advisor, you will be asked to enter a password, and a hint to help you remember it. (If you forget it, you'll have to reinstall Internet Explorer if you ever want to change the Content Advisor!)

Many respectable and very useful sites – including the BBC – have no rating

# Adding a rating system

You can make Content Advisor more effective by adding other ratings systems. At the time of writing, there is only one other system in general use, and that is from SafeSurf. It has different rating categories to those of the default ICRA system, but is otherwise used in the same way.

1. Open Content Advisor and switch to the General tab.

2. Click **Find rating systems**. This will link you to the Content Advisor support page at Microsoft's website where you will find a link to SafeSurf.

3. At SafeSurf, click the Update Your Browser link. Download SafeSurf.rat, their ratings file, storing it in your Windows/System32 folder.

4. Close the SafeSurf window.

5. Back at Content Advisor, click **Rating systems...**.

6. At the Ratings System dialogue box, click **Add**.

7. At the Open dialogue box, select the SafeSurf file – it may take a while to find the file.

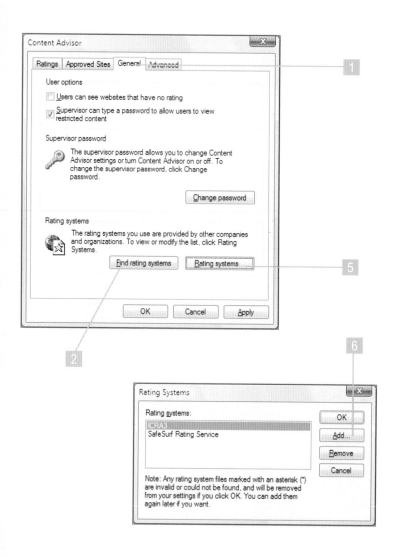

I'm not quite sure why this is in the same tab as Content Advisor, as it's a very different aspect of the system. AutoComplete tries to do your typing for you. It watches when you type a web address or enter details into forms, and tries to complete it for you, offering up addresses or words that you have typed before and which start with the same letters. It's quite a handy feature, especially with web addresses.

◀ **Configuring AutoComplete**

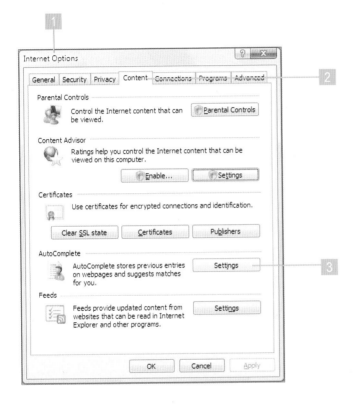

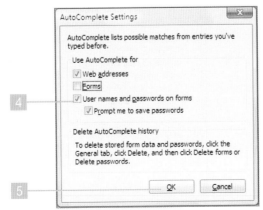

1 Use Tools, Internet Options... to open the Internet Options dialogue box.

2 Switch to the Content tab.

3 Click Settings .

4 Turn on AutoComplete where you want it. It's certainly useful for web addresses and the user names and passwords option may prove to be handy, depending upon how you use the web.

5 Click OK .

4

# Configuring the Connections

The main option on the Connections tab is how Internet Explorer should manage the dial-up connection. You can set it to dial-up for you whenever a connection is needed – i.e. when you type or click on the address of a web page that is not stored in your temporary Internet files folder, or when you start to send an email. There are two versions of this option: one for those working on a local area network, the other for single computer users.

The alternative is 'Never dial a connection', which leaves it up to you to start the dial-up connection when you want to go online.

Automatic dialling will normally save a bit of bother but can occasionally be a nuisance. There will be odd times that it sets off when you don't want it to, but it's simple enough to cancel.

If you are testing a new Internet service provider, or have a second account as a student or through work, one of the connections must be set as the default.

1. Use Tools, Internet Options… to open the Internet Options dialogue box.

2. Switch to the Connections tab.

3. Select a dial option.

4. If you have more than one connection and want to change the default, select it and click [ Set default ].

5. Click [ OK ].

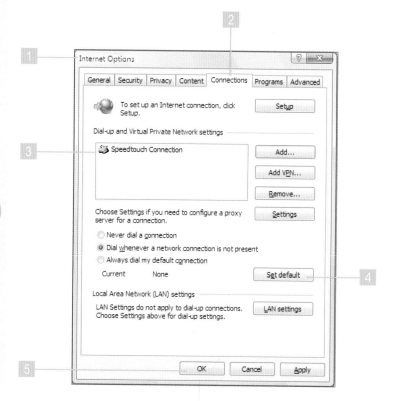

**For your information**

If you have a second connection and want to use that instead of the default, activate it through its desktop shortcut or Start menu entry before you start Internet Explorer.

There are over fifty options here! They can, of course, all be left at their defaults, and I would recommend that you wait until you have been browsing for a few weeks before you touch any of them – with the exception of the very first two. If you have the screen set to high visibility, you should turn on these Accessibility options at an early stage.

When you feel ready, there are two sets of options that you can adjust. The Browsing options tweak the way that Internet Explorer works. Experiment with these – none can do any harm.

The Multimedia options control the display of sounds and graphics. You can choose whether or not to play sounds, animations or videos – all of which are purely decorative but add to downloading time. If you have a standard phone connection, not broadband, then turning these off, especially video, will result in faster browsing. You can opt not to show images, which will speed up your browsing but will make it impossible to view those sites that use images to hold their links.

If you want to use the Image toolbar, turn it on from here – it's near the top of the Multimedia set of options.

## Setting the Advanced options

1. Use Tools, Internet Options... to open the Internet Options dialogue box.

2. Switch to the Advanced tab.

3. Scroll through the list. If you are not clear about the effect of an option, leave it at its default setting, otherwise turn it on or off to suit yourself.

4. Click ⬚OK⬚.

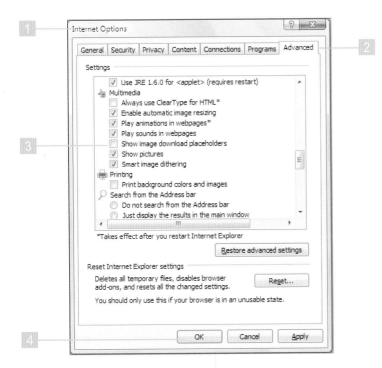

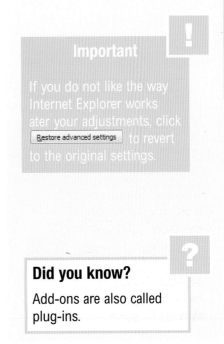

**Important**

If you do not like the way Internet Explorer works after your adjustments, click ⬚Restore advanced settings⬚ to revert to the original settings.

### Did you know?

Add-ons are also called plug-ins.

# Managing your add-ons

Browsers can display only formatted text and GIF and JPG graphics. Add-ons extend the range of files that they can handle. These are extensions to the browser, not independent applications. Some are supplied as part of the package, others can be downloaded from Microsoft or other sources when they are needed. No add-on is essential, but some are widely used. As a minimum, you should have the Java platform, QuickTime, RealPlayer, and Flash Player.

1. Use Tools, Internet Options... to open the Internet Options dialogue box and switch to the Programs tab.

2. Click Manage add-ons to open the Manage Add-ons dialogue box.

- Java is a programming language used in web pages.

- QuickTime, from Apple, is the leading video player, and can also handle audio files and streaming formats.

- RealPlayer handles streaming audio and video and is widely used for live broadcasts over the web.

- Flash Player, from Macromedia, is much used for animated multimedia displays and for games.

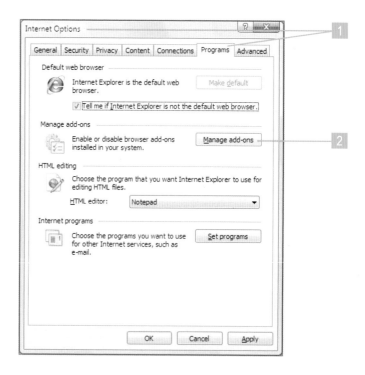

**Did you know?**

Add-ons are also called plug-ins.

3

**Manage Add-ons**

View and manage add-ons that are installed on your computer. Disabling or deleting add-ons might prevent some webpages from working correctly.

Show: | Add-ons currently loaded in Internet Explorer ▼ |

| Name | Publisher | Status | Type |
|------|-----------|--------|------|
| Disabled (1) | | | |
| Yahoo! Toolbar | Yahoo! Inc. | Disabled | Toolbar |
| Enabled (5) | | | |
| Adobe PDF Reader Link Helper | Adobe Systems, Incorporated | Enabled | Browser H |
| Yahoo! Toolbar Helper | Yahoo! Inc. | Enabled | Browser H |
| Research | | Enabled | Browser E> |
| SSVHelper Class | Sun Microsystems, Inc. | Enabled | Browser H |
| Sun Java Console | Sun Microsystems, Inc. | Enabled | Browser E> |

◀ [========= III =========] ▶

**Settings**

Click an add-on name above and and then click Enable or Disable.

○ Enable
◉ Disable

**Delete ActiveX**

Click the name of an ActiveX control above and then click Delete.

[ Delete ]

Download new add-ons for Internet Explorer

Learn more about add-ons

[ OK ]

4     5     6

3 Open the Show list and select Add-ons currently loaded...

4 If you see an add-on that you know you never use, select it and click Disable in the Settings area.

5 If there is a disabled add-on that you need again, select it and click Enable.

6 Click [ OK ].

4

**Did you know?**

You can also reach this dialogue box from the Tools menu by selecting Manage Add-ons...

# Installing add-ons

Whenever you meet a file that needs an add-on, it will normally be accompanied by a link that you can use to get the software. Exactly what you have to do to download and install the add-on varies, though the process is almost always straightforward and there are usually clear instructions. Here, for example, is what happens when you install RealPlayer.

1 You will be alerted when you need an add-on, and you will be offered a link to a site from whence you can download it. Follow the link.

2 At the site, read the instructions. If there are different versions of the software, choose the one for your computer system.

3 At some sites, including Real, there will be a special program which you run to download and install the software. Click Run to start.

4 At other sites, you download the software onto your PC then install it from there. Click Save, then pick a folder to store the file – use Downloads or any folder that you can find again easily. Do not change the filename!

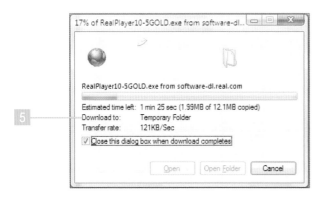

5 Wait while the file downloads. If you have a normal (56k) phone connection, this could take a while!

6 Installation may start automatically. If it does not, go to the folder in Windows Explorer or Computer and double-click on the file to start the installer.

7 You may be asked to confirm the installation.

8 You may be asked to configure the software to your system. Set the options to suit, leaving at their defaults any that you do not understand.

4

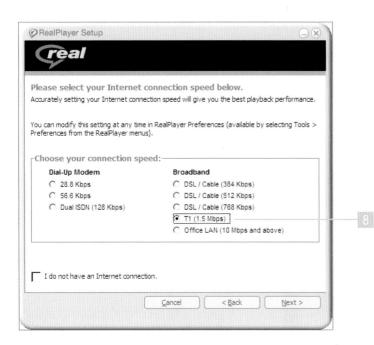

# Getting Adobe Reader

Adobe Reader is one add-on that you really should have. This is what you need to view and print PDF documents. People use PDFs for information booklets and advertising brochures, for books (this one went to the printer's as a PDF) and for paper sculpture kits (see below) – in fact, for any document where well-formatted text and images are needed. PDF stands for Portable Document Format, and it is portable. A PDF file can be viewed on any computer or printed on any printer and the result will be the same.

1 When you try to open or download a PDF file you should find a link to get the Adobe Reader 'Plug-in'. Click it.

or

2 Head directly to Adobe at www.adobe.com and follow the links to get the Reader.

3 Follow the instructions to Download and install the Reader.

4 When you next come across a PDF file, Reader will start up inside Internet Explorer. Use its toolbar buttons to save, print or do other work with the document.

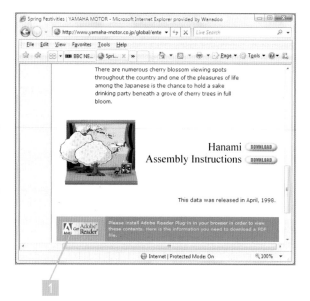

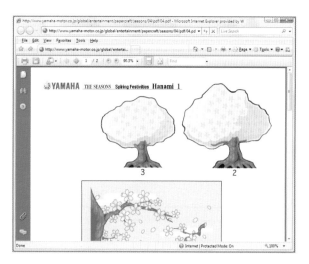

## Did you know?

Yamaha Motor Company have some lovely paper model kits (in PDFs) for free downloading – great for the grandkids on rainy afternoons! Find them at www.yamaha-motor.co.jp. Search for 'papercraft' and follow the links.

Add-ons are one way for browsers to handle files that they cannot display themselves; an alternative is through linked applications. When you open a file of the relevant type, its application is then opened inside Internet Explorer. It may run in a separate window in the main display area, or it may be merged into Internet Explorer, with its commands added to the menu bar. Among the applications that can be linked in this way are Word, Excel and other Microsoft Office programs.

## Using a linked application

1. Look for any changes in the menu bar or toolbars.

2. Check out any new buttons to see what extra facilities they hold – e.g. when Word is linked, this button is added ⛁. If you click on it, the standard Word toolbars will appear.

3. Use the linked application's commands to edit, save or print the document.

4

# Searching the web

## Introduction

If you can find a good start point on a topic, you can usually follow it through from page to page using the hypertext links that they so often contain. People writing on a topic will very often refer you on to other pages – their own or other people's – to find out more about particular aspects of the topic or related matters. However, with so much information spread over so many pages on so many sites over the web, the problem is where to start. And it's not just a matter of quantity – there is no quality control on the web. Anyone can publish anything, and no one checks it for accuracy, relevance or even literacy. So the question isn't so much 'where can I find something about this?' but 'where can I find something worth reading about this?'

Directories and search engines offer different solutions. In a directory, selected web pages are organised into a catalogue – a hierarchy of topics and sub-topics. In a search engine, pages are scanned and key words are stored in a database; this is searched by keyword, and matching pages are listed. The difference in the way that links to pages are gathered has an important effect on the quantity and quality of the results.

In practice, many of the sites that started life as directories now offer search facilities; most of the search engine sites now have directories within them; and most Internet service providers offer directory and search facilities at their sites. In this chapter, you will meet a selection of sites that offer one or other or both types of facility for finding material on the web.

## What you'll do

**Understand directories and search engines**

**Understand search techniques**

**Search Google**

**Run an advanced search**

**Search for images at Google**

**Search from Yahoo!**

**Search the web at AltaVista**

**Turn on the AltaVista family filter**

**Use the Excite directory**

**Use Ask**

**Ask for directions**

**Search the web at UK Search**

**Browse from UK Net Guide**

**Find a business at Yell**

# Understanding directories and search engines

## Directories

All directories contain sets of links, organised into a hierarchy of categories and sub-categories. They are always compiled by humans (as opposed to the 'spiders' used by search engines).

There are a few where every linked page has been viewed and assessed by someone from the directory. Though this reduces the number of links, it does improve quality control – all the pages linked from these have some merit. Some enlist the help of volunteers to review and recommend pages. Others are largely compiled by self-submission, relying on those who created the web pages to select the appropriate place in the directory's hierarchy. Descriptions of contents are also produced by the pages' authors. Clearly you don't have the same guarantee of quality, but even here directory staff have to enter the information into the directory and some minimal selection will still be taking place.

Unless the directory has an automated system for checking the links, they will gradually go out of date, so expect some dead ends.

## Search engines

You can find most things by browsing through directories, but it can take a while – especially if you are researching an esoteric topic. This is where the search engines come into play.

Search engines vary in the way they build their indexes of the web, but they all use some kind of automated system. They have 'spider' programs that steadily work their way through the web, sending back information on the pages they find. Some will only pick up selected items from web pages – typically the title, anything listed in the meta-information, plus labels for images and text from the top few lines; others scan right through the page. Some will only read the top page at any site; others delve into every page.

Because these are automated systems, there is no quality control in building the index. However, most search engines try to assess the usefulness of a page, by some form of analysis on the content or by calculating how many links at other sites point to a page, or by other measures. These assessments are used when displaying the results of a search, so that the most promising links are listed at the top.

## Important

No search engine can offer a 100% coverage of the web, as pages are being added and changed constantly. If you don't find what you want at one, it is often worth trying another.

## Jargon buster

**Meta-information** – information written into HTML pages for the benefit of spiders, but not visible on screen – see page 266.

Most search engines allow you to define searches in similar ways. The techniques listed here will work at all the major (and most other) search engines.

## Keywords

■ Use the roots of words for maximum effect; boat will find 'boats' and 'boating' – 'boats' may not find variations on the word.

■ If you give several words in a simple list, a good search engine will list first those pages that contain all the words, followed by those that contain some or only one of them.

## Refining searches

Multiple keywords can be joined by special symbols or the words AND or NOT to define the relationship between them.

■ If words are written in "double quotation marks", the engine will search for an exact match of that phrase; e.g. "never so few" will find pages about the film of the same name. Without the quotes, these words may find relevant pages, but they will also turn up a lot of totally irrelevant stuff. For people's names and commonly linked words, the quotes are not really needed.

■ + or AND specifies that both words must be present; e.g. 'boat +wood' (no space between + and the following word) or 'boat AND wood' will find wooden boats, boats made of wood, as well as the Boat Inn at Fleetwood and other things you didn't want!

■ – or NOT specifies that pages containing the following word are not wanted; e.g. 'goldfish –card' or 'goldfish NOT card' when you want the things for your pond, not your wallet.

5

### Timesaver tip

Most search engines have an advanced search facility where you can define the search more closely, e.g. setting date limits, selecting the language or the country of the page's website.

## Searching Google

1. Go to Google at www.google.co.uk.

2. Enter one or more words to define year search.

3. If you only want local sites, check the Pages from the UK option.

4. Click Google Search .

Google is the leading search engine. It has a phenomenally large database – over 8.1 billion web pages at the time of writing, but its searches are staggeringly fast, finding results in a fraction of a second. It uses a ranking technique to rate sites, based on how many links point to a page, and where they come from. If a high-ranking site has a link to a page, then it is worth more than a link from a less important site. Pages are also relevance-rated on the basis of where the search keywords appear in them. If the words are in the title and/or occur several times within the text, it is likely to be more relevant than a page where the words only occur once. These ratings are combined to order the results list, so that the most promising links are displayed in the top section of the page.

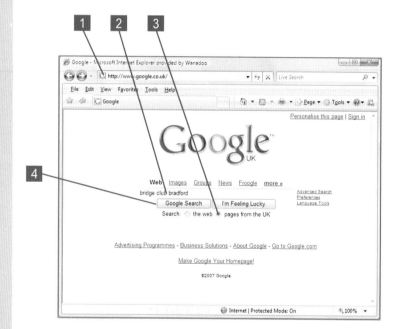

Usually, the best way to get a good set of relevant links is to be as specific as possible in your choice of keywords. In the example here I'm looking for a bridge club in Bradford. Is there one? Does it have a website? Google will soon tell me.

The resulting page has the Bradford Bridge Club right at the top of the main listing. It also has a link to another bridge club in Bradford plus – and this is the clever bit – links to other bridge clubs in the area. It recognised that Bradford was a place and did a geographical search as well.

5  Read the brief descriptions to select a page.

6  Click on the title or the address to go to a page.

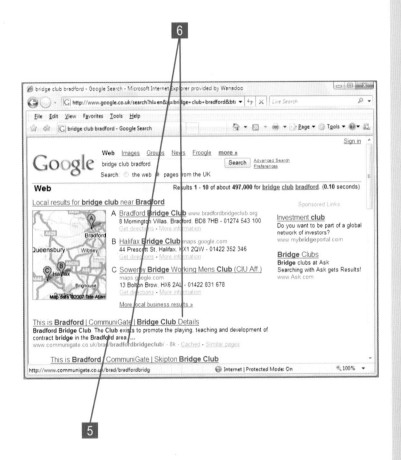

## Important

The main Google website is at www.google.com and this works just as well for many searches. However, if you want the results optimised for the UK, use google.co.uk.

## Searching within the results

1 Start a new search as normal.

2 When the results appear, go to the bottom of the page and click the Search within results link.

3 Enter more keywords.

If you do not define your search tightly enough, even the best ranking system will still produce far too many results. No problem, there is a simple solution – at Google you can run a search within a set of results. In fact, narrowing your search by stages can be one of the easiest ways to find things. If you define the search very closely at the start, there is a danger of being so restrictive that you miss a lot of potentially interesting stuff. And the more complicated that you make a search, the greater the chance of typing errors. Keep life simple.

In the example below, I'm trying to track down a copy of *Honeysuckle Rose* by Fats Waller. Search for a song by your favourite artiste, or for something else that you can look for in at least two stages.

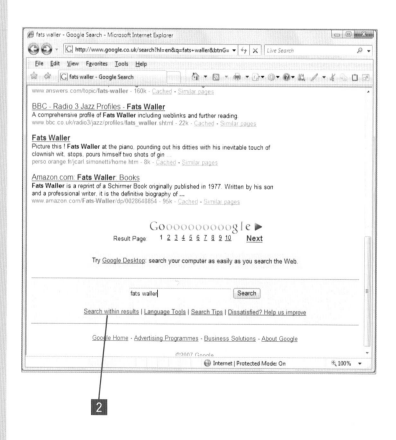

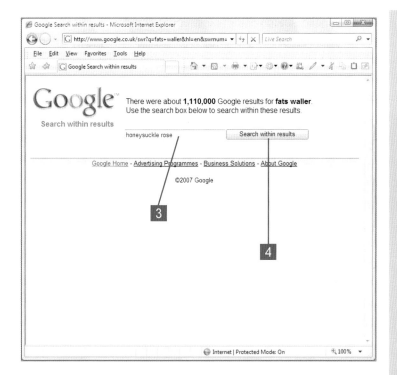

**4** Click Search within results.

**5** Check the results. Has this brought suitable pages to the top of the list?

**6** If you are still getting too many, and you need to narrow the search further, repeat steps 2 and 3.

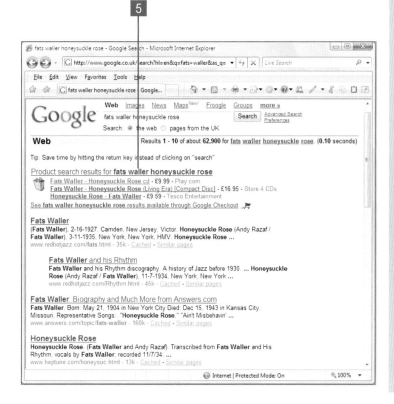

## Timesaver tip

At Google – as at most search engines – the results will normally include sponsored sites. Companies can pay to have their sites listed when a search may relate to their products or services. Ignore these if you are just looking for information.

5

# Running an advanced search

The advanced search routine lets you define the keywords more precisely, but more importantly it allows you to specify things which you cannot control in a simple search. These include the newness of the material, its language, and the file format – Google doesn't just find web pages, it also finds documents linked from web pages, and sometimes the format matters.

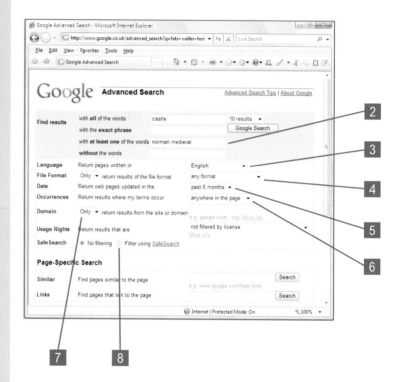

**1** Go to Google, and click the Advanced Search link by the Search box.

**2** Define your keywords, and the relationship between them, i.e. which words must or must not be there, and which can be there.

**3** Set the Language.

**4** To restrict the File Format, select Only (or Don't) at the start of the line, then the format to include (or not) from the drop-down list.

**5** If only newer results are wanted, set the Date limit.

**6** If you think it might help, select from the Occurrences list where the words should appear on the page.

**7** If you want to restrict the search to a domain, e.g. '.uk', type it in.

**8** Turn on SafeSearch if you want to filter the results.

The standard search at Google gives you links to web pages. You can also search for:

- Images – these are embedded in web pages, but may not show up in a standard page search.

- Groups – places for people to meet online to discuss common interests.

- News – searches the sites of the press, TV and other media.

- Froogle – a price-conscious shopping search for the frugal.

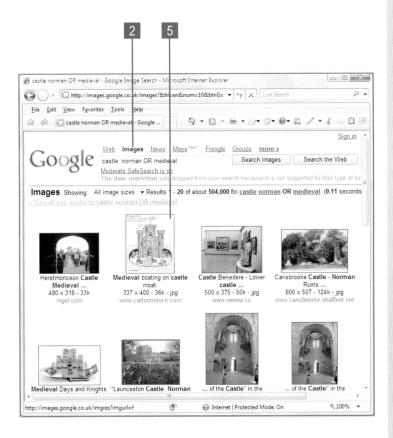

**1** Go to Google at www.google.co.uk

**2** Select Images.

**3** Enter one or more words to define your search.

**3** Set the Pages from the UK option if required.

**4** Click [ Google Search ].

**5** Click on the thumbnail of an image to open its web page.

### Important

Google is much more than just a search engine. Spend some time there and dip into its news services, listen in on or join a group, or see if you can find a bargain at Froogle.

5

# Searching from Yahoo!

1 Go to Yahoo! at uk.search.yahoo.com.

2 Type into the Search slot one or more words to define what you are looking for.

3 Select where to search – all the web or just the UK or Irish sites.

4 Click on Web Search.

5 Click on a page title to go to a linked page.

Yahoo! made its name as a web directory, and it is still probably the best around, but if the directory fails, or you don't know where to start looking in it, there is also a search facility.

The basic Yahoo! search produces results from the web in general, though it does seem to favour pages which are also listed within its directory (a good move, as these have been quality checked). With these pages, it shows their Yahoo! category and gives a link to it. You can either follow a link to a web page, or you can go to the category and explore further within Yahoo!

If you start a search from within a category listing at Yahoo! you can choose to limit the search to links within that category, rather than the whole web. Obviously, you will get far fewer results, but they do have the Yahoo! seal of approval.

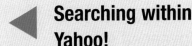
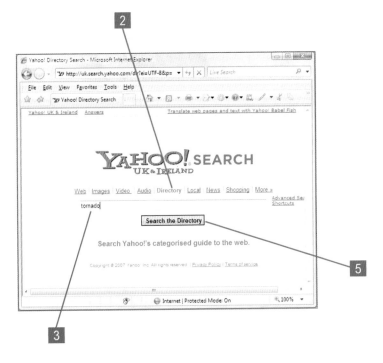

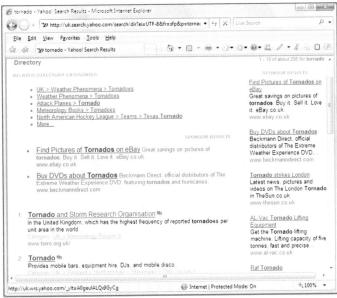

1. Go to Yahoo! at uk.search.yahoo.com.
2. Click the Directory link above the Search box.
3. Enter your search words.
4. Select This category only.
5. Click Search the Directory .

## Timesaver tip

If you don't know which category to start from, you can search the entire directory. This will still be restricted to Yahoo! links. Take the Yahoo! web Directory link on the top page at step 2, and select the Directory at step 4.

5

# Running an advanced search

The advanced search routine at Yahoo! is similar to the one at Google. The main difference is that here you can restrict the format to HTML, i.e. web pages – an option that is surprisingly absent from Google, where HTML is not in the list of formats.

A second difference worth noting is that you can specify that the search words must be in the title or the URL of a page. This can be very handy when you are trying to find a site that you visited some time in the past, and can remember part of its title or address.

1 Go to Yahoo! and click the Advanced link by the Search box.

2 Enter the words to look for or to avoid.

3 If you want to search only the title or URL – not just in any part of the page – select this from the list.

4 If you want to limit the search to one domain, select it or type it in.

5 To restrict the File Format, select the format from the drop-down list.

6 Turn on SafeSearch if you want to filter the results.

7 Click [ Yahoo! Search ].

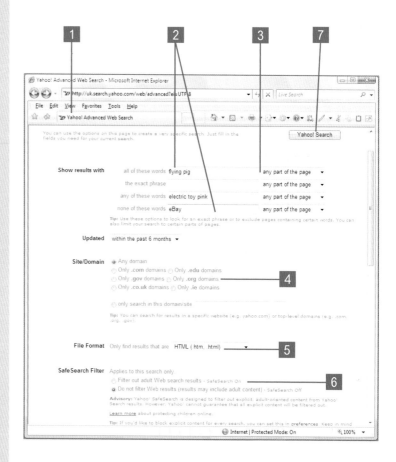

AltaVista was one of the first great search engines, and though it has now been eclipsed by Google, it is still a good place to hunt for links. It has a few special features worth noting:

■ You can search for images, audio recordings, videos and news as well as for web pages in general.

■ You tend to get more text about each page than you do at Google.

■ There is a 'family filter', which we will come back to on the next page.

1 Go to AltaVista at www.altavista.com or uk.altavista.com.

2 Enter your search words.

3 If you only want UK results, limit the search to United Kingdom.

4 Click **FIND**.

5 Follow up any interesting links.

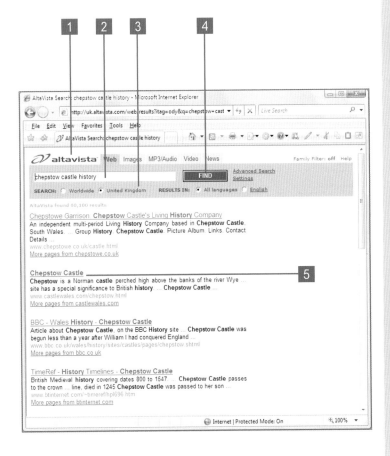

# Turning on the family filter at AltaVista

If you turn the family filter on before the grandchildren come to stay, there shouldn't be any nasty surprises in the sites that AltaVista finds for them.

You can set it to filter everything, or just multimedia – videos, images, etc. If you want, you can protect the settings with a password, though I'm not convinced that this is worth doing. If the people you are trying to protect are capable of trying to change the settings, then they are equally capable of going to an alternative – unfiltered – search engine.

1 At AltaVista, click Settings next to **FIND**.

2 Below the Family Filter heading, click the Change link.

3 Set the level of filtering – or remove it if the grandchildren have gone home!

4 Click Save Your Settings.

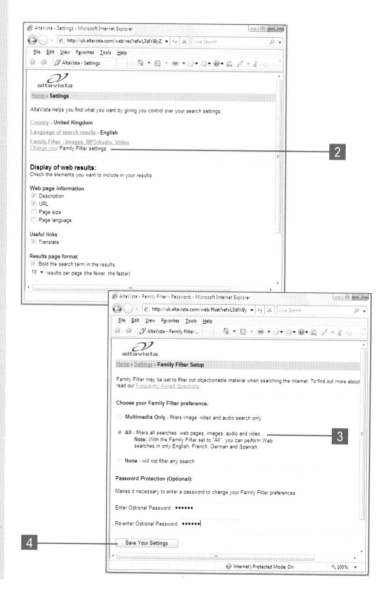

As you will see in the next chapter, most newspapers, TV and radio stations now have websites where you can find out the latest news, so why is the news search routine at AltaVista worth looking at? Three reasons:

- It will take you directly to the reports on any topic and this could well be quicker than trying to locate the story at a news media site.

- It will find reports on matters of limited interest that may not make it into your preferred news site.

- You can get a fuller view on what is happening by reading several reports from different sources.

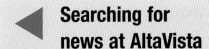

## Searching for news at AltaVista

1. Go to AltaVista at www.altavista.com or uk.altavista.com.

2. Select News.

3. Enter your search words.

4. If it will help to focus the search, select the topic.

5. Pick a region, if desired.

6. Set the date limit.

7. Click **FIND**.

8. Follow up the links.

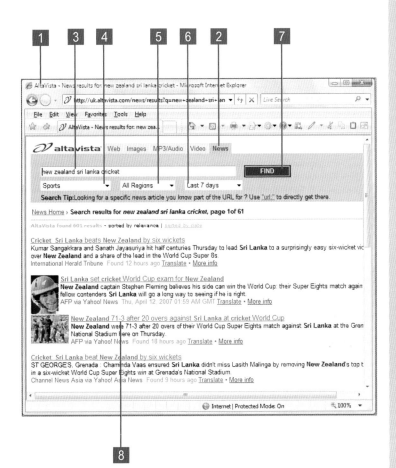

5

# Using the Excite directory

Excite offers regular news, weather and share reports, gossip, horoscopes and a range of other services. It also has an extensive directory, which is why we are looking at it now. The directory is organised into a hierarchy of categories, as at Yahoo! As you work through the hierarchy, you will find that each page has a set of related sub-categories listed at the top, and links to websites beneath. The deeper that you go into the structure, the more of each page will be devoted to site links.

As a general rule, the Excite directory is more informative than Yahoo!, with concise descriptions of each site.

1 Go to Excite UK at www.excite.co.uk.

2 In the Directory area, click a heading or subheading.

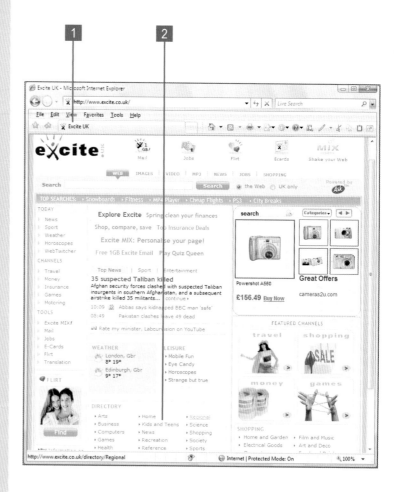

## Important

The Excite directory is part of the Open Directory project, a network of volunteers who each maintain or contribute to a small part of the catalogue. In practical terms, this means that all the linked pages have been read and assessed by someone, and the links are more up to date than at some other directories.

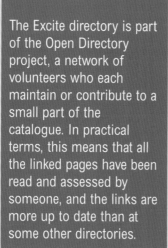

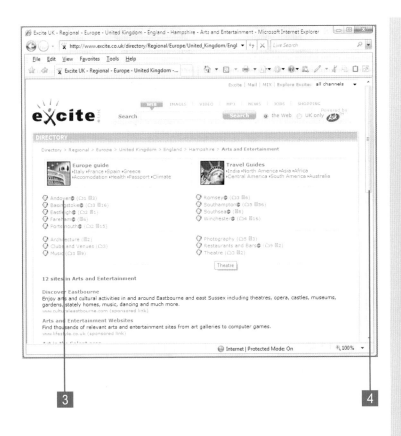

3 If you want to go deeper into the hierarchy, click on a sub-category heading.

4 When you reach the desired level, scroll down to view the links.

5 Click on the page title to go to a page.

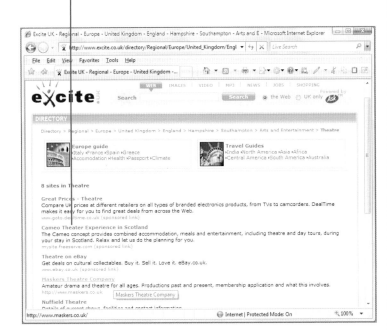

## Timesaver tip

When you follow a link from Excite, the page opens in a new window. This means that you can go back to the old window to follow up other results from the search – just remember to close the windows after you have finished with them.

5

## Searching at Excite

▶

As well as the directory, Excite provides a very good search engine. As at Google, there is a huge database, but the ordering routine ensures that the most promising results are displayed at the top of the list.

If a standard search brings up too many irrelevant results, the advanced search will let you specify words to avoid, and to limit the domain and the language – but that's as far as it goes.

**1** Go to Excite search at www.excite.co.uk.

**2** Enter two or three words to define your search. (My blackcurrants are suffering, and I'm hoping that Excite will help me to find a cure.)

**3** Click on Search.

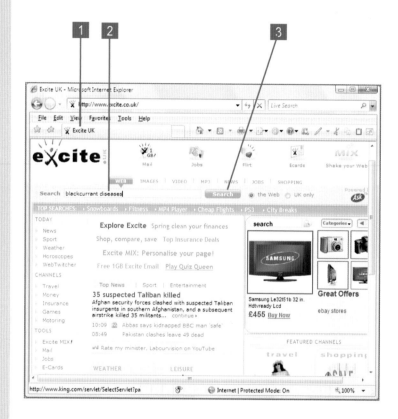

If a standard search at Excite produces little of use, you can carry the search across to Ask. Look for the link at the bottom of the results page.

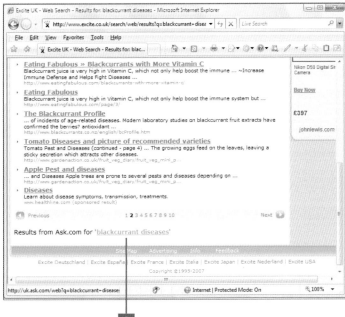

4 Read through the summaries of the results to see how closely these match what you are looking for. In this case, the links are to pages about diseases of blackcurrant bushes and to how blackcurrants can help fight diseases. I should have included 'bush' or 'plant' in the search words.

5 Click a title or URL to follow up a link.

6 If you don't get what you need, go to the bottom of the page and click the link to take the search to Ask.com.

5

# Using Ask

▶

Ask is optimised to answer questions of the 'Where can I buy...' variety. You can use it to search for information, and it will serve that purpose very well, but what it does – and probably does better than any other search engine – is track down products and services. It even has a Products search option, which we will come back to in the next chapter when we look at shopping on the web.

1 Go to Ask at www.ask.co.uk.

2 Enter your keywords.

3 If you are looking for local sites, select Search UK webpages only.

4 Click Search .

5 The first few links will usually be to sponsored sites. These may be worth investigating if you want to buy, otherwise scroll down the list.

6 Click a page title or address to follow a link.

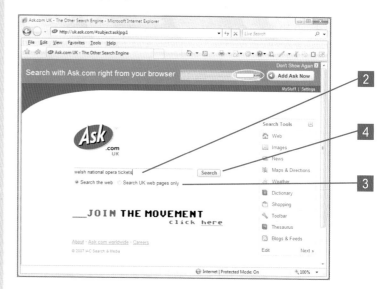

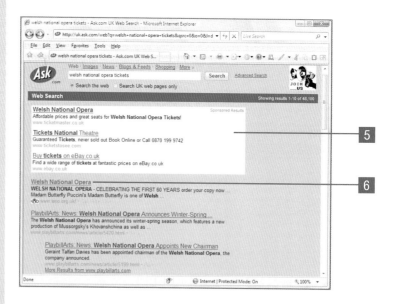

## Did you know?

Ask has a save option that lets you save your search for later reuse. This may be handy sometimes.

Ask has map and direction facilities on its site. They are easy to use and nicely presented. To get directions, you just give the start and end addresses – postcodes avoid ambiguities, but it can cope with street and town names instead – and off it goes.

I never cease to be impressed by how rapidly these route finders can work out how to get from one place to another, no matter where they are. The results for car journeys are always good. The On foot ones are more variable as the system doesn't know enough about footpaths or public transport.

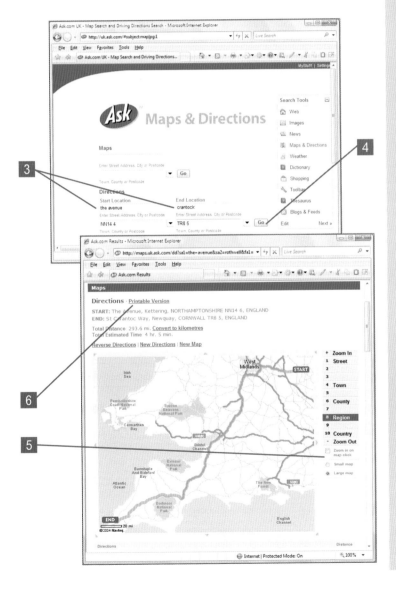

## Asking for directions

1. Go to Ask Jeeves at www.ask.co.uk.

2. Click the Maps and Directions option.

3. Enter the Start and End addresses as accurately as you can – use postcodes if you can.

4. Click Go.

5. To get a detailed map of part of the route, select Zoom in on the map, then click on the part you want to examine.

6. To get a print out, click Printable version and print from there.

5

# Searching the web at UK Search

The Yahoo!, Excite, AltaVista and Ask sites covered here are the UK versions of websites that have their main base in the USA. This does not detract from their value – the directories are all clearly UK-focused, but retain an international core. UK Search is different. It started in the UK and its results are centred on UK sites.

There are five different routes you can take to find links at UK Search: web, Regional, Sectors, Advanced and Directory. We'll start with the search.

**1** Go to UK Search at www.uksearch.com.

**2** Make sure that 'web' is selected.

**3** If what you are looking for is listed in the quick searches, click on it.

otherwise

**4** Enter your search words.

**5** Click **SEARCH**.

**6** Read the extracts for the sites and click the names to follow the links.

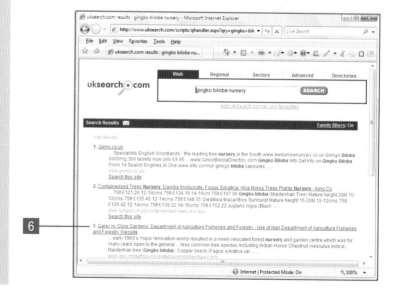

## Timesaver tip

If you want to define your search more closely, use the Advanced routine, where you can specify which words to include, which to avoid and which are essential.

The Regional search centres the results on any selected area, listing first those suppliers or organisations based in, or with branches in, the area. I like it as an idea, but it has limitations at the time of writing. It should become more useful as more local businesses set up websites and as more of these are added to the directory.

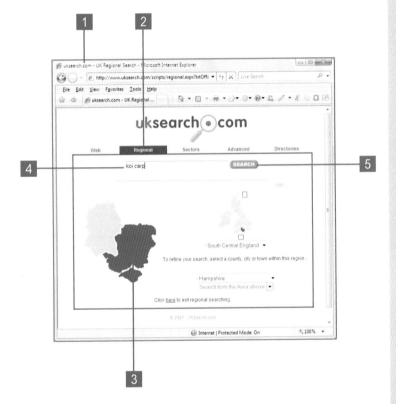

## Searching your area at UK Search

1 Go to UK Search at www.uksearch.com.

2 Select Regional.

3 Click on the UK map to select a region, then click on a county or city.

4 Enter your search words.

5 Click **SEARCH**.

6 The results will be listed with those from your chosen area first, followed by those from surrounding counties.

### Did you know?

In the Sectors at UK Search, you can search selected sites in health, education, shopping and finance.

## Browsing from UK Net Guide

UK Net Guide takes a bright, friendy, magazine-style approach, though with a good, wide-ranging directory beneath its surface. This has around a dozen sections, all of which have the same basic features, including: links into the directory; 'guides' giving explanations or advice about relevant matters; searches on related topics; an 'answerbank' – an interactive space where people can ask for help or discuss issues.

1 Go to UK Net Guide at www.uknetguide.co.uk.

2 Click on a tab to select a section.

3 Click on a Search link if there is a suitable one for you.

or

4 Type what you are looking for in the Search box and click Go. This will give you a list of the relevant categories in the directory and a selection of sites from the wider web.

or

5 Click on a heading in the Category list to get into the directory.

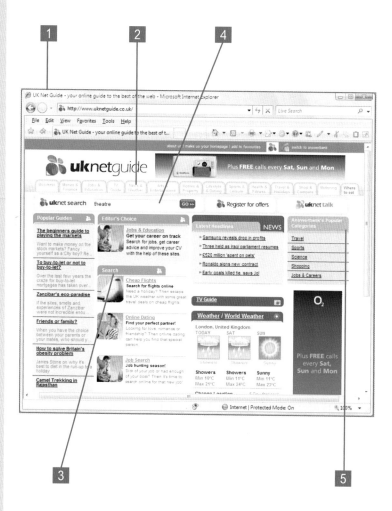

A notable and useful feature of UK Net Guide is that it has editorial comments on all the sites that it lists, sometimes with a star rating. A moment checking the comment and rating can save you time downloading sites that you then decide are not what you really want.

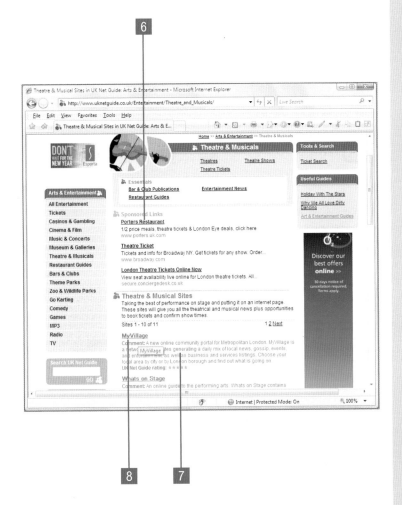

**6** Scroll past the sponsored links to see the site listings.

**7** Read the comments for any likely sites, and check the rating, if given.

**8** Click on the name to go to a page.

## Timesaver tip

UK Net Guide is a good place to start shopping. There are lots of useful links to retailers and you can compare prices.

5

## Finding a business at Yell

Yell is a directory, not a web directory, but I've included it here as it's not to be ignored.

Yell is the online version of the Yellow Pages telephone directory. It is organised in the same way, but with a few more features. You can search for a business by name or by type, and the listings include email and website addresses if present.

**1** Go to Yell at www.yell.com.

**2** Enter the type of product or service, or the company's name.

**3** Enter the town or city.

**4** Click SEARCH .

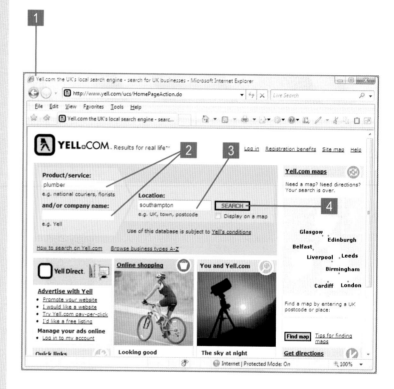

**5** Work through the results to find suitable leads.

**6** If required, click the Map/Directions link to find out how to get to the business.

**7** If there is a Save to address book link, you can use this to get an email address. Note that you must register with Yell to be able to use this service.

5

# Internet resources

## Introduction

The Internet is a tremendous source of knowledge, but it's not so much a treasure house of information, as a gold mine – there's a wealth of nuggets, but you have to dig them out for yourself!

This is not as daunting as it may sound. If you look in the right places, the gold-to-tailings ratio is high, and in any case, you get to see some good scenery while you are prospecting. So, grab your pick and let's get going before this metaphor gives

# Looking up a word in a dictionary

## Look up a word in the Oxford Dictionary

**1** Go online and head for Ask Oxford at www.askoxford.com.

**2** Type the word into the Search slot.

**3** Click on Go.

**4** Read the definition.

Many of the 'standard' reference books are now available online. Amongst others, Britannica, Encarta and Hutchinson's encyclopædias, Webster's dictionary, the Oxford and Cambridge dictionaries, and Roget's Thesaurus. The normal practice at most of these websites is to allow free access to a limited amount of information – the basic definition of a word or a brief encyclopedia entry. If you want the full text, with images and maybe video and audio as well, then you have to become a paying subscriber. At Oxford Reference Online, for example, £95 (+VAT) a year buys access to an impressive range of reference books, though not including the Oxford English Dictionary – that will cost you another £195 (+VAT). Fortunately, the free site does the job for most of us!

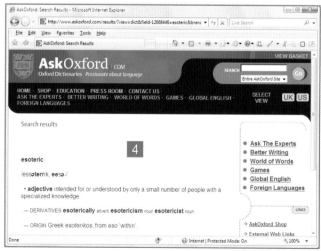

Don't understand what the kids are talking about? Here's the answer – the Dictionary of English Slang. Apart from its inherent usefulness, I've included this as an example of a purely online dictionary – you can't buy a printed edition – and also as an example of the things people do purely for the love of it. This dictionary is maintained by Ted Duckworth, and fortunately, there are a lot of people like him, who greatly add to the richness and variety of the Internet.

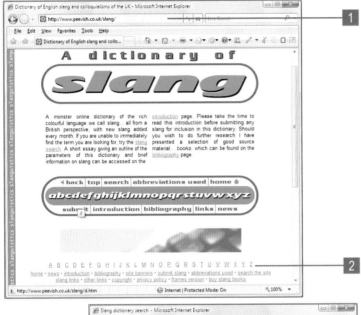

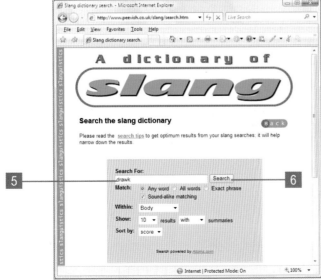

### Look up a word in a slang dictionary

**1** Go to the Dictionary of English Slang at www.peevish.co.uk/slang.

**2** Click on a letter.

**3** Scroll through the listing to find a particular word – or just browse through and marvel at the richness of our ever-developing language!

or

**4** Click on the Search link at the bottom of any page.

**5** Type in the slang word that you want defined.

**6** Click Search .

### Timesaver tip

The search can be slow – browsing is often quicker, and more fun.

# Discovering Wikipedia

This is a unique collaborative venture that has produced a superb resource – and one that continues to get better every day. At Wikipedia anyone can create an entry or edit an existing one, which may sound a slapdash approach to building an encyclopedia, but is actually far from it. There's a real commitment to accuracy here. All entries and edits have to be backed up by references, where possible, and a host of critical eyes check every addition. If errors do find their way in, they are not there for long!

1 Go to Wikipedia (in English) at en.wikipedia.org.

2 Click a heading link to browse through the articles.

or

3 Type into the Search box the name or item that you want to look up.

4 Click on Go.

5 Cross-referenced items are in blue – click to read their articles.

6 If you want to read how the page evolved, switch to the Discussion tab.

7 If you have something to contribute, take time to read around the site – especially the Help pages – before you start.

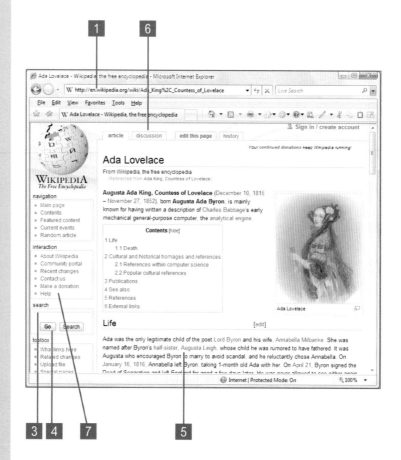

Streetmap gives you what you might expect from its name – and more. You can get a detailed street map for any town in the UK, plus road maps – at a variety of scales – and, sometimes, aerial photos. You can locate a place by name, postcode, Ordnance Survey or Landranger reference, latitude and longitude or even telephone code! You can then use its 10km scale road map to plot a route to the town, and a 500m street map to find your way to the house.

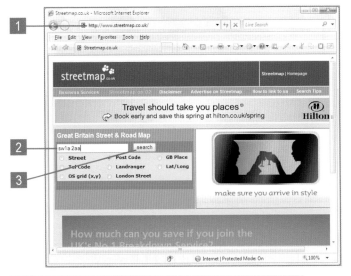

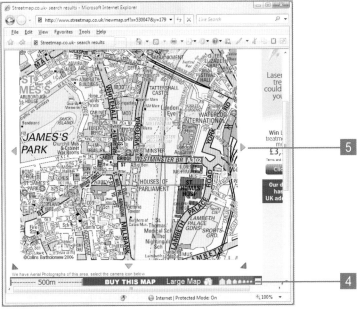

1 Go to Streetmap at www.streetmap.co.uk.

2 Enter a place name, postcode or other identifier.

3 Click Search.

4 Click the zoom controls to change the scale.

5 Click the arrows around the edge to scroll over the map.

## Timesaver tip

Postcodes work best!

# Getting a route from the RAC

The RAC has a very neat route planner. It will give you a detailed route between any places in the UK or Europe, telling you exactly when to turn and which road to take next. Which is all very clever, but it is the interactive map which is the most fun. You can take an overview, go in closer to see the road numbers or town names, or focus right in to street level, and then move around the map at that level of detail.

**1** Go to the RAC site at www.rac.co.uk.

**2** For a route between two places in the UK, enter the From and To street addresses or postcodes.

**3** Click Go ▶.

**4** For a more complex route, or one into Europe, click the Advanced route planner link and enter the From and To addresses.

**5** The route will be given as detailed instructions, and as an interactive map.

## Did you know?

The AA also offers a first rate route planner at its website www.theaa.co.uk. Try them both and see which you prefer.

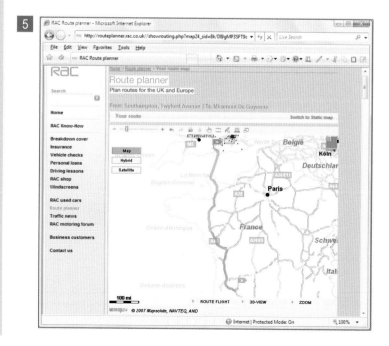

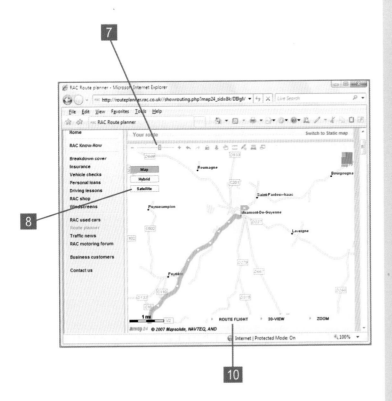

6 To zoom in on part of the map, draw a rectangle around it.

7 Use the zoom slider to get a close-up of an area.

8 Click Satellite to get a satellite photo of the map area.

9 To get a print out, click Printable version and print from there.

10 Click Route Flight to "fly" the route!

The instructions are very detailed and clear.

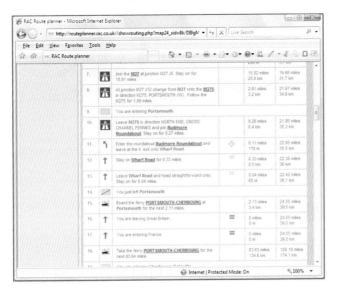

# Getting advice from NHS Direct ▶

Feeling poorly? Don't know whether it's worth bothering the doctor – even if you can get to see one in the near future. Why not check out NHS Direct's self-help guide. It may well be able to give you a likely diagnosis, and suggest a course of action. There are three possible suggestions:

This will be accompanied by a care routine.

Sometimes you need to speak to a person.

Double-check your symptoms, then ring!!

1. Go to NHS Direct at www.nhsdirect.nhs.uk.
2. Click the Self-help guide link.
3. Click the Body key link.

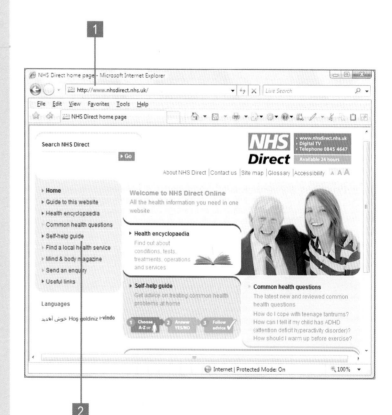

## Did you know? ?

You can also look up symptoms in an alphabetical index.

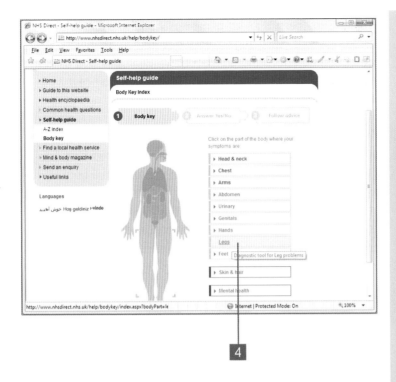

**4**

**4** Use the chart or the list to identify the location of the problem.

**5** You will be offered a set of options for that area. Select one.

**6** You will be asked a series of Yes/No questions to help diagnose the problem. Keep working through until you get an answer.

**7** Follow the advice!

**6**

# Finding a book at Project Gutenberg

1. Go to Project Gutenberg at www.gutenberg.org.

2. Follow the Online Book Catalogue link.

3. If you want to see what's there, try browsing by author – they are grouped alphabetically. Click on a letter to get a list, then scroll through.

4. The available titles by each author are listed after the names. Click on a title to start downloading. (Go to step 7.)

Project Gutenberg is an on-going collaborative effort to put literature online. They currently have around 17,000 works by over 1,000 authors, ranging from David Phelps Abbott to Edward Huntington Williams, with Thomas De Quincey, Herodotus and Beatrix Potter in between.

The books are stored mainly as plain text, with some as Word documents or HTML pages, and normally in zipped files. Compressed text does not take much space – a full book will typically make a zip file of 200 to 300 Kb, which will download in 2 or 3 minutes even on a standard dial-up line. When you've got the text on to your machine, you can read it on-screen or print it out. For sheer convenience, a paper copy may be worth the time and cost of printing it out.

Go over to Project Gutenberg, and explore. As there are so many books, you must expect to spend a while browsing the shelves, but it's all nicely organised and downloading is straightforward – just follow the instructions.

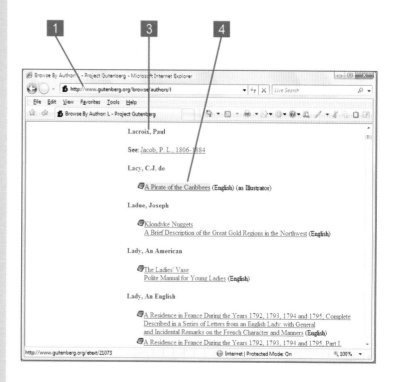

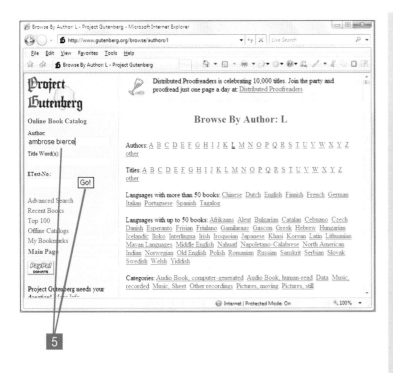

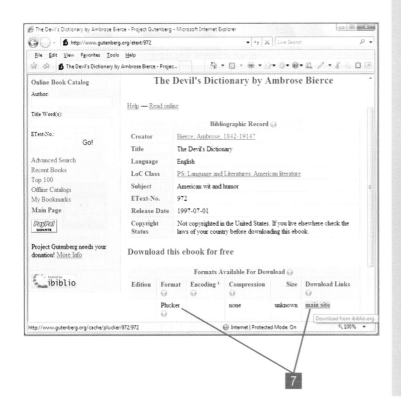

5   If there is a particular author or book that you want, go back to the Online Book Catalogue page, type in name or title in the search area and click Go!.

6   A search for an author will give you a list of titles. Select one if you want it.

7   You will normally be offered a choice of formats, and of places to download from. Pick the zip file for the fastest downloading.

8   Many books are also available from mirror sites. If you have trouble downloading from the main site, cancel and try from one of the mirror sites.

## Jargon buster

**Mirror site** – one that holds the same files, organised in exactly the same way as at the main site. Many popular file stores have mirror sites.

# Reading the papers

Most directories and portals carry some news and sports results, but if you really want to read the news, then you should turn to the papers. All the national papers and many of the local ones now have sites, and these normally carry the same stories and range of features as the printed editions.

## Jargon buster

**Portal** – website that aims to be central to how people use the web, by providing a range of services and activities, such as a directory, search facility, games, email and chat rooms. The hope is that users will start each browsing session from that site and come back to it regularly. ISPs usually run their sites as portals for their members.

## Important

While the papers all give free access to their news coverage, they may restrict some special reports and other services to subscribers, e.g. if you want to get to the *Times*' or *Guardian*'s crossword online, you'll have to cough up £25 p.a.

The *Telegraph* (www.telegraph.co.uk) was the first of the UK nationals to go online with its Electronic Telegraph. It has now been joined by the *Times* (www.timesonline.co.uk), the *Financial Times* (news.ft.com), the *Guardian* (www.guardian.co.uk), the *Daily Mail* (www.dailymail.co.uk), the *Mirror* (www.mirror.co.uk), the *Sun* (www.thesun.co.uk) and many more besides.

Like all the national papers, *The Guardian* makes all its news reports available online. And there is more than just today's news at hand – you can search back through the archives to fill in the background of stories if you are trying to catch up. As the archives (of all the papers) build over the years, they will become an increasingly valuable tool for historical research.

But online access should not be just another way to read your favourite paper. It can also be a way to read the ones you wouldn't – or couldn't – normally see. If you want to practice your language skills, you can read the foreign press – the national papers are online in just about every country. If you want to be able to keep up with the news in your home town, you may well be able to read the local paper online.

First find your papers! Here are three ways to locate sites:

■ If you sometimes read the printed paper, look in a copy for its web address.

■ Go to Google, type in the paper's name and – if it is a UK paper, select the UK only option.

■ Go to www.wrx.zen.co.uk/britnews.htm where you will find a comprehensive set of links to newspaper sites. This is good for local papers.

It is always interesting to compare the front pages of the papers on any given day, to see what are the most important things in their different world views – and you can do this easily online.

# Watching TV at the BBC

1 Go straight to the newsroom at news.bbc.co.uk

2 Follow the link to watch the news on video.

or...

All the TV companies now have their own websites, which they typically use to tell people what's coming, or to give the background or more details of current programmes. Some do far more. The BBC's website is one of the most popular UK sites, because it is not just an extension of their standard broadcasting. This is an education, entertainment, analysis, news and sports resource of the highest quality. One of its features that I find most useful is the up-to-the-minute news. You can view the most recent news broadcast at any time, or follow up individual stories – many with live audio/video feed.

Visit the BBC's main site at www.bbc.co.uk or go straight to the newsroom at news.bbc.co.uk.

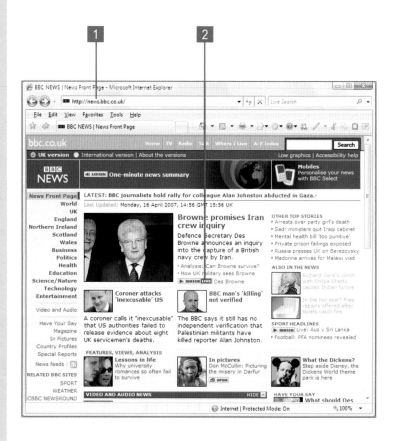

## See also

You can watch videos at the BBC site using either Real Player or Windows Media Player. Real Player may produce slightly better quality viewing, but you will need to download and install the player from Real. There are links at the BBC site that will take you there. For more on installing Real Player see page 100.

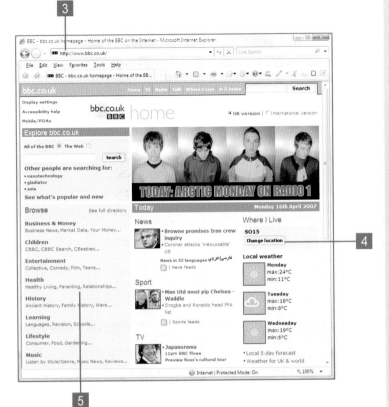

# Watching TV at the BBC (cont.)

3   Go to the BBC's main site at www.bbc.co.uk.

4   Set the 'Where I Live' location to your postcode to get local weather and links to local news and stories.

5   Browse the directory to find the stories behind and arising from programmes.

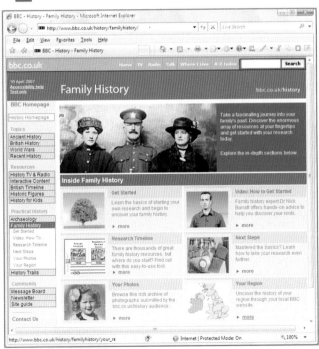

# Listening to BBC radio

1 Go to the BBC at www.bbc.co.uk.

2 Click the Radio link at the top of the page.

3 At the radio home page, select a station.

Radio stations have been 'broadcasting' over the Internet for some years now, but it has only been since the widespread take-up of broadband that they have really taken off. You can listen to the radio online through a standard phone line, but the quality is not that great and there are too many breaks in transmission – especially if you are also trying to go to other sites at the same time. Radio broadcasts are normally in either Real Player or Windows Media Player formats, or both, with the former more widely used. If you want a good choice of stations and programmes, you need Real Player.

There are several ways to find radio stations. BBC stations are easy to find.

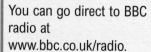

## Did you know?

You can go direct to BBC radio at www.bbc.co.uk/radio.

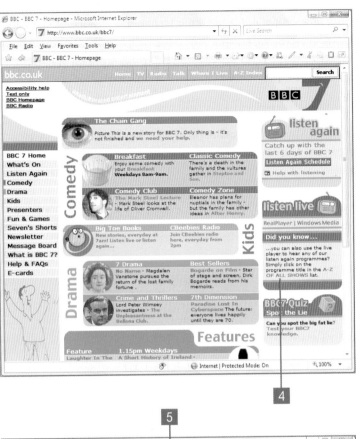

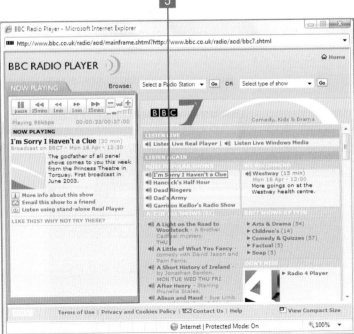

**4** The station's page will give you a lot more than just what's on. But somewhere there will be a link to take you to the broadcasts.

**5** At the station's Radio Player page you can listen live or pick up stored broadcasts – from recent programmes and material from the archives.

## Important

The first time at the site, you will be offered a choice of formats – Real Player or Windows Media Player. Real Player is the best choice at the BBC site as far more material is broadcast in that format.

# Tuning the radio in Media Player

Media Player doesn't just play radio broadcasts, it can also be used to locate stations on the Internet, through its built-in link to the Windows Media centre. Internet Explorer does not need to be running to use the player, and if it is running, it can be completely independent, so there is one online connection direct to the player, and another to the browser.

As with any form of online radio, this works much better on a broadband connection.

1 If you have been listening to the radio already, the player may be running. If not, open the Start menu and run Media Player from there.

2 Click the Media Guide button, then, when you are online to Windowsmedia.com, select Radio then Radio Tuner.

3 Use the search routine to locate a station, or ...

4 Pick one from the featured list.

5 Click the arrow at the right of a station to open its options.

6 Click Play.

7 Media Player will connect to the station's website and start to broadcast. It will also display the site's home page.

8 If you want easier access to a station in future, click Add to My Stations.

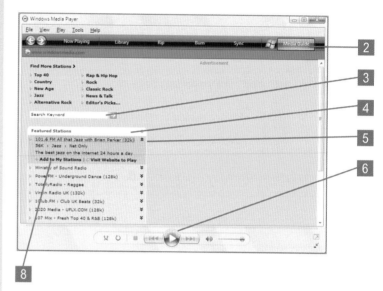

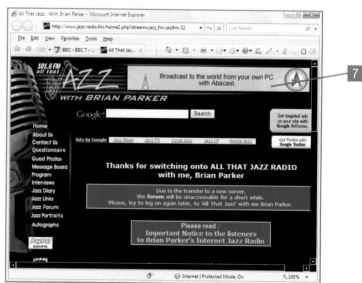

And one more way to locate a radio station – this time through Internet Explorer. The Radio-Locator site claims to have just about every online station in its listings. I'll believe them – they found 364 in the UK alone. Some stations are very local, very specific and none the worse for that. I think it's rather nice that you can use this world-spanning network to tune in to your local hospital radio.

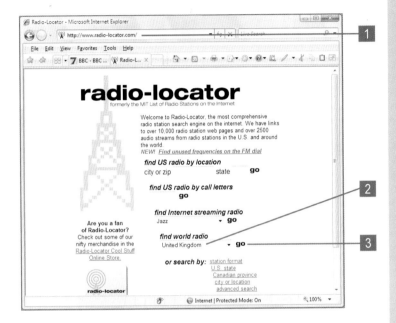

1   Go to Radio-Locator at www.radio-locator.com.

2   You can search by US city, US radio call sign, music format (e.g. jazz, rock, classical, etc.) or world radio by country. Type or select an option in the appropriate box.

3   Click **go**.

4   Select a station from the list – there may be several screens of them!

| Info | Call Sign | Frequency | City | Format | School |
|---|---|---|---|---|---|
| ⓘ | Northsound Two | 1035 AM | Aberdeen | Unknown Format | |
| ⓘ | Oak 107 | 107 FM | Loughborough | Variety | |
| ⓘ | Oasis FM | 96.6 FM | St Albans | Unknown Format | |
| ⓘ | Ocean FM | 97.5 | Portsmouth | Hot AC | |
| ⓘ | OneWord | National Digital | London | Unknown Format | |
| ⓘ | Panjab Radio | Satellite | London | Unknown Format | |
| ⓘ | Passion Radio | internet only | Brighton | Dance | |
| ⓘ | Peak 107 | 107.4 | Chesterfield | Adult Contemporary | |
| ⓘ | phoenixfm.com | Internet only | Brentwood | Adult Contemporary | |
| ⓘ | Plymouth Sound | 97FM | Plymouth | Variety | |
| ⓘ | Power FM | 103.2 FM | Southampton | Unknown Format | |
| ⓘ | Premier Christian Radio | | London | Unknown Format | |
| ⓘ | Premier Radio | 1305 AM | London | Religious | |
| ⓘ | PRFM | Internet | Cambridge | Dance | |
| ⓘ | PrimeTime Radio | National Digital | London | Unknown Format | |
| ⓘ | Pulse | 97.5 & 102.5 | Bradford | Unknown Format | |
| ⓘ | Pulse Radio | 87.7 FM | London | Alternative | London School of Economics |
| ⓘ | Purgatory FM | | Hull | Top-40 | |
| ⓘ | Pyrotechnic radio | | London | Dance | |
| ⓘ | Q102 | 102.9 FM | Londonderry | Unknown Format | |

### Important

Once you have connected to a site to listen to it you can browse elsewhere without breaking the connection.

# Buffing up on a movie

If you love movies, you'll love the IMDb – the Internet Movie Database. This has the credits, plot, trivia, goofs, stills and reviews from pretty well every movie ever made, in the whole world, not just the USA and Europe, since the dawn of movie-making. Use it to get the lowdown on a film, to track an actor's career, or to answer 'What did we see her in last time?'

1  Go to the IMDb at www.imdb.com.

2  Select the search mode – you can search by titles, names, characters, companies or other aspects.

3  Enter the name or title.

4  Click go.

5  Everything is cross-linked. In a movie listing, click the cast and crew link to go to their pages. Actors' pages list their movies – click to go to one.

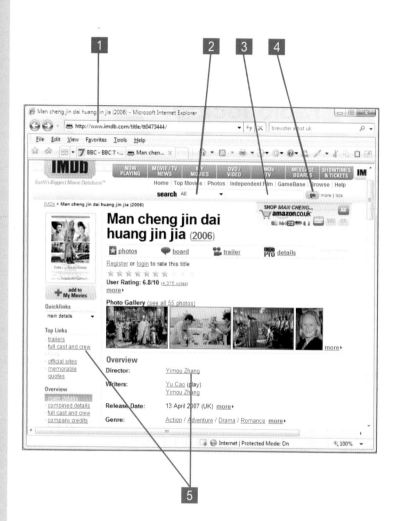

The IMDb can tell you pretty well everything you might want to know about a movie – except where you can see it! Still, finding what's on at your local cinema is not difficult. You can tackle the question from two ends: either use a local information site, or go to the websites run by the cinema chains, and ask about your local one there. Let's take the local information site route.

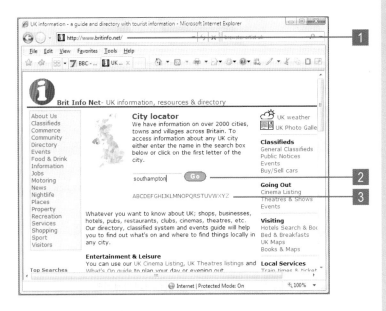

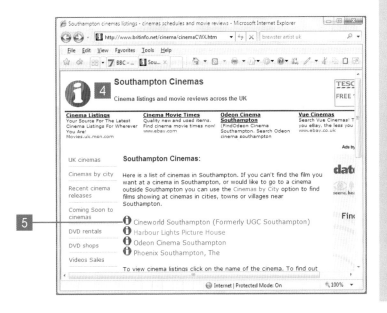

1 Go to Brit Info at www.britinfo.net.

2 Type a town and click 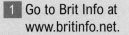.

or

3 Use the A-Z listing to locate the town.

4 At the town site, select Cinema Listings.

5 Click on the cinema to get details of the showings.

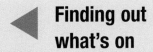

## Did you know?

All the cinema chains run sites where you can find out what's on and book your tickets. Here are a few of the biggest:

www.cineworld.co.uk

www.odeon.co.uk

www.picturehouses.co.uk

# Visiting the Tate

Many museums and art galleries have a website, using it to advertise their exhibitions and opening times – and perhaps to try to sell you something from their gift shop. The more active ones also use their sites to extend the experience or to provide background information for their exhibitions. The Tate is one of the most active, with having put its entire collection online – or rather notes and images of its collection. It also provides good information about exhibitions, has an extensive Tate Learning area and stages online events regularly. Go to the Tate and find out more!

1 Go to the Tate Online at www.tate.org.uk.

2 Click the picture links to find out about the main events.

3 To get background information about other current, past or future exhibitions, select one from the drop-down list.

4 To explore the 65,000 pictures in their collection, click the Tate Collection link. Selecting by artist or theme will bring you to a set of pictures – and there may be anything from 2 to 2,000 in a set.

5 Browse through the pictures. If you select one, you can read its notes and/or see a bigger image of it.

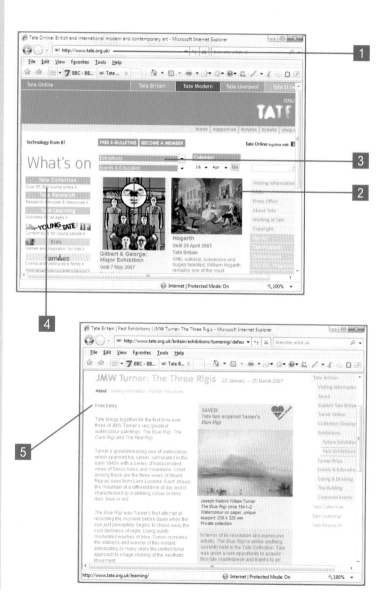

The Web Museum is not a museum. It is an art gallery designed for the web, an unfunded project started by Nicolas Pioch and grown with the help of volunteers, with the aim of making art more accessible to a wide audience. The pictures are shown as thumbnails, grouped by theme and artist, and accompanied by thoughtful biographies and artistic commentaries. These thumbnail images are all linked to much larger ones – sometimes full-screen. The quality is clearly not as good as you would get in a good art book, but the images are larger, and clearer than those at Tate Online.

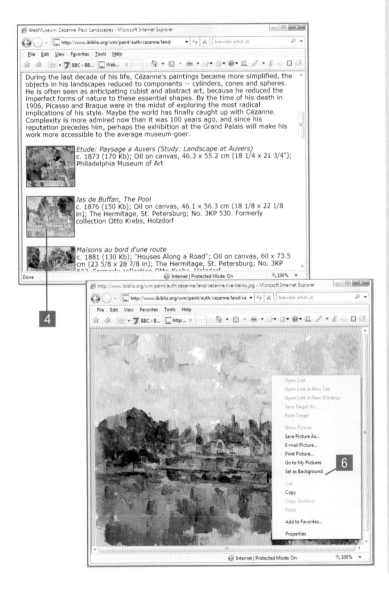

1 Go to the Web Museum at www.ibiblio.org/wm.

2 Visit the special exhibition of Cézanne or the medieval art of the Duc de Berry.

or

3 Go to the Famous Artworks collection and pick a theme, then an artist.

4 If you want to get a better view of a picture, click on its thumbnail.

5 If the picture is a big one, press [F11] or open the View menu and select Full Screen for a bigger viewing area.

6 If you really like a picture, right-click on it and select Set as Background, to put it on your desktop.

# Downloading shareware

The Internet is a great source of free or cheap software, largely distributed through the shareware sites. One of the best of these is download.com. What makes it so good? There's lot of choice; the programs are reviewed so you know what you are getting; the programs are checked for viruses – so you know you are not getting more than you asked for! There are two main categories of software:

- **Freeware** is there for the taking. People give software away for a variety of reasons, but just because it is free does not mean it is no good. Internet Explorer is freeware!

- **Shareware** can be tried for free, but you need to register and pay the fee (typically around £30) to continue to use it. Among the many excellent shareware programs are WinZip, the standard file compression utility, and Paint Shop Pro, one of the leading graphics packages.

## Important

If you only download files from established websites, you should not have any trouble with viruses, as these sites check files for viruses before accepting them. For extra safety, install antivirus software on your PC and check your downloads.

Downloaded software will usually come in one of three forms:

- **Ready-to-run programs** – just click and go! If you intend to keep the program, move it out of the temporary folder on your hard drive into safer storage.

- **Standard Zip files** – if you have Windows Vista or XP, you can open these in Windows Explorer, which treats them as compressed folders. If you have an older version of Windows, you will need a copy of WinZip to unpack them. These sometimes contain the program and associated files in ready-to-run form, but often have a set of installation files, and you must then run the Setup or Install file to get the actual program.

- **Self-extracting Zip files** – these have been created by WinZip, but have the unpacking routines built into them.

When you run a self-extracting Zip file, or unpack an ordinary Zip file, their constituent files will normally be unpacked into the same folder. If these are the program files, you may want to set up a new folder for them and move them into it. If they are installation files, you will be prompted to choose a folder for the program during installation. The installation files can then be deleted from your temporary folder.

2 In the Search field, enter the
name of a program or words
to describe the type of
software, e.g. 'graphics
animation'.

3 Click Go.

4 If you get too many results,
select the Advanced search
and set the OS (operating
system) or other filters to
narrow down the selection.

5 When you get the results,
select the Advanced search
and read the brief descriptions
to identify the file you want.

6 Click on the Download Now
icon. You will be taken to a
new page to select a download
site – pick one geographically
close to you, as closer
generally means faster
downloading.

7 Select Save to disk, then
choose a folder to save it in.

# The interactive Internet

## Introduction

On the web you will find many sites that are designed to be used actively and interactively. You can shop, find a house (and fix up a mortgage for it), insure your car, play games, make new friends and so much more. It is impossible to list all the services that are now available on the web – there are just too many, with new ones appearing all the time. In the UK alone, thousands of firms large and small now provide information, offer services or sell their goods over the Internet.

### Is it safe to bank and shop online?

The Internet has its fair share of crooks, but if you observe a few sensible precautions, you should be able to buy online as safely as you can by mail order or in the high street.

- It is cheaper to trade on the Internet than on the high street or by mail order, so you should expect to get a better deal, but if an offer sounds too good to be true, it probably is!

- Don't deal with people you don't know. If a firm is new to you, check that they exist by looking them up at Yell (uk.yell.com) or the Companies list at Yahoo!

- You are as safe paying by credit card over the Internet as you are over the phone – which is not completely safe. Check that the 🔒 icon is present in the status bar – this shows that your transactions with the site are secure.

- Security should not be a problem with established high street banks, which use secure systems and have reputations to protect. But do watch out for emails that claim to be from banks and want to check your details. No banks ever do this!

# Buying a book at Amazon

1. Go to Amazon's UK branch at www.amazon.co.uk.

2. Drop down the Search list and select Books.

3. Type the title or author into the Search slot.

The web is a good place to sell anything which people buy on specification rather than by trying on, e.g. computer hardware and software, books and CDs. It is also a good place to sell those specialist goods that can be difficult to find in your local high street – organic foods, collectors' items, or almost anything handmade. Compared to a high street shop a web retailer is likely to offer a wider choice of goods, and you can browse at your leisure for the best buy; but you can't try things for size or feel their quality, and returning goods can be expensive in postage.

At Amazon, they have in stock, or can quickly get, just about every book that's in print. Finding books is simpler here than on the shelves of a high street shop – and now you can even browse some of them in the same way! The quick search will normally do the job, but there is also a full search where you can hunt by author, title, ISBN, publisher and other features. Like most web stores, Amazon uses a 'shopping basket' approach. After you have added all your items, you head for the checkout. There you register with the store, giving your credit card and contact details – you should only do this once. On later visits, only your name and password are needed.

**4** You will see a list of matching – and almost matching – books. There may be a lot of them! Scroll through to find the one you wanted.

**5** Click on the book name if you want to know more about it, read the synopsis, customer reviews and sample pages (if available).

**6** To buy, click

Add to Shopping Basket .

**7** Continue shopping or, click

Proceed to Checkout to buy.

**8** The first time through you will have to set up your account. As a returning customer, you just give your email address and password.

**9** At the checkout, check and change the order if desired.

Click Place your order to end.

You will get an order confirmation by email within the hour. And your books should be there within the week!

# Shopping at Tesco

In the UK at present, the biggest online retailer is also the biggest supermarket – Tesco. Their success is well earned. Their site is simple to use, with timesaving shortcuts if you are in a hurry, and they can deliver to anywhere within range of most of their stores. There is a charge of around £5, but it's worth it for the convenience if you don't have the time, energy or transport to visit the store. Allow yourself half an hour for your first visit to Tesco online. Apart from registering, you'll need to spend time finding your way round. Subsequent shopping trips can be much faster as you can leap to your favourite products, or use a typed list for a very quick shop.

1. Go to Tesco online at www.tesco.com.

2. Select a part of the store, e.g. groceries.

3. You will be asked to log in. The first time you will need to give your contact/delivery details and set a password. Next time, you just type your email address and password to log in.

4. Start shopping! To browse the 'aisles', click a department button.

5. Select a category, then a sub-category – and possibly a third-level sub-group.

## Did you know?

You can also buy your groceries online at these (and other) sites:

www.sainsbury.co.uk

www.waitrose.com

www.iceland.co.uk

www.fortnumandmason.com.

# Shopping at Tesco (cont.)

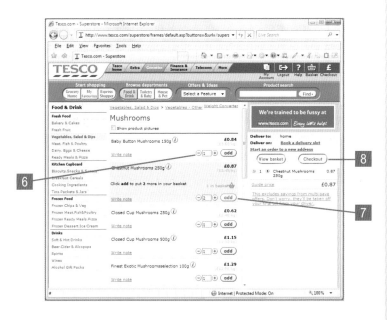

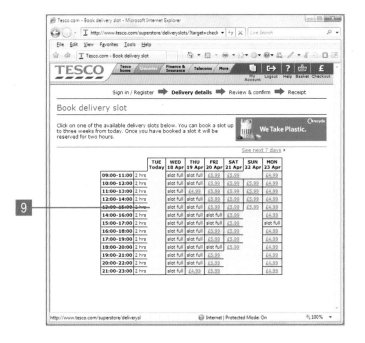

**6** A list of items within that category will appear. Find the one that you want, and use the ⊕ and ⊖ buttons to adjust the number.

**7** Click add to add the items to your basket.

Repeat 3 to 6 as necessary.

**8** Click Checkout when you have done.

**9** You will be asked to book a 2-hour delivery slot. Find one that suits best.

**10** At the checkout, you confirm the order and payment.

## Timesaver tip

Regular shoppers can store their shopping lists and then simply do repeat orders before looking for any special, different items.

# Finding a bargain at Kelkoo

We've already noted that one of the key advantages of web retailing is lower prices. Several web companies have built on this idea and will search for the best prices for you.

Kelkoo is currently the leader in this field. Their well-organised site offers an efficient search facility that will tell you where on the web you can buy an item, and at what price. They also have some good gift ideas at Christmas!

1 Go to Kelkoo at www.kelkoo.co.uk.

2 Select a category, then work through the following pages to identify the exact item.

or

3 Type what you want to buy and click Search .

4 Check the results to find the best deal. Click the Store info link to find out more about the retailer.

5 Click Go to go to the store to buy the item.

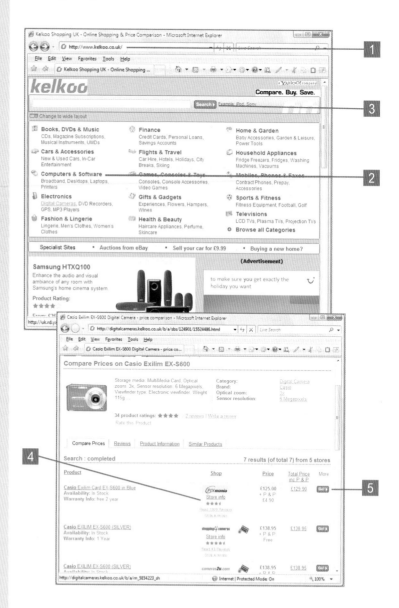

Time for a new motor? If you need help deciding what car, then a good place to start is *What Car?*'s website (www.whatcar.co.uk) where you can read reviews and compare prices and performance.

If you are looking for a new car, every car manufacturer has a website where you can get the specifications of their range, and details of promotions, and where you can set up a test drive, or at least link to a local dealer.

If you are looking for a used car (or a new one), start with a trip to *Autotrader*'s site, which has an excellent database of new and used cars. Use it to locate a dealer or private seller in your area.

1 Go to Autotrader at www.autotrader.co.uk.

2 In the Quick Search area, define the car and give your postcode.

3 Click Search .

4 You will be given a list of matching cars within 50 miles of your postcode. Click on the links for contact details and for more about the car. (I'm looking for a Cooper, to replace my ageing Mini.)

**Timesaver tip**

The address of a company's site is usually www.firm.co.uk, where firm is 'ford', 'citroen' or whatever. If this doesn't work, type the firm's name into Google – that'll give you the address.

# Booking a coach trip

You can book just about any kind of travel tickets online – planes, boats, trains and coaches! Some of the providers have had teething problems in developing their services, but nowadays online booking is almost always straightforward and reliable. What I like about it is that you can check times and prices without having to commit to booking at that moment, so you can find out your options before you make your final plans.

The example here is National Express, but the process would be very much the same if you were booking train tickets at National Rail Enquiries (www.nationalrail.co.uk) or at the Trainline (www.trainline.com).

**1** Go to National Express at www.nationalexpress.com.

**2** Pick your From and To points from the short lists (or use the longer lists for more off-the-track journeys.

**3** Enter the journey dates.

**4** Click **TIMES & FARES**.

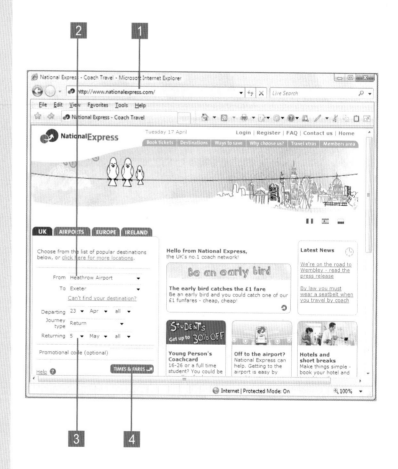

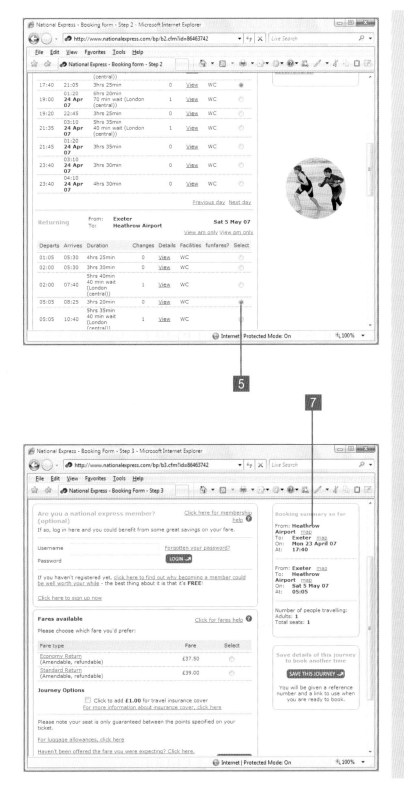

**5** You will be given a list of possible journey times. Select the outward (and return) times that suit best.

**6** Scroll down the page to specify how many tickets are needed, and for whom – don't forget that there are special rates for the over 60s.

**7** At the booking summary page, check the tickets and times. If you are or may become a regular coach traveller, become a national express member – join up now. If you are already a member, log in.

**8** Click ⟨CONTINUE⟩ to order the tickets and pay for them.

# Planning a holiday

1. Go to Expedia at www.expedia.co.uk.

2. Select the Flight/Hotel/Car combination you need. We'll look for a full set.

3. Enter the dates and airports of your intended flight. (There may not be flights on that route on those dates, so be prepared to return to here to try an alternative route.)

4. Choose a hotel. If the suggested flight and car are both suitable, click Choose and continue. Otherwise…

5. Click Change flight.

You can plan your holidays online – the whole thing, from car parking at the airport through to the day out in the fishing boat, with the flight, hotel and car hire in between. You will get a flexibility that you will not find in many travel agents, and at good prices. Very occasionally, paying deposits may be a minor hassle. Most places take credit cards, but sometimes they'll need a wire transfer instead – and that means a trip to the bank to set it up, and you don't have quite the security of a credit card transaction.

You can make all your bookings through different sites, but you may find that you can plan the total package through Expedia.

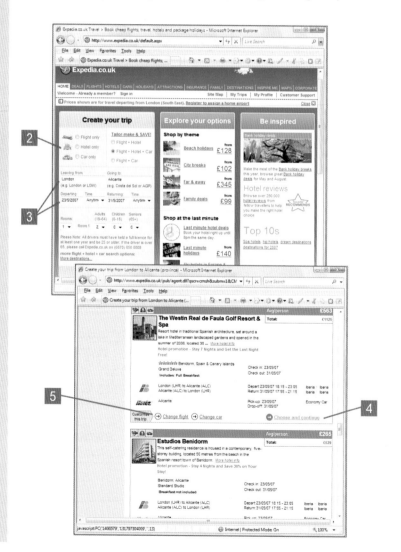

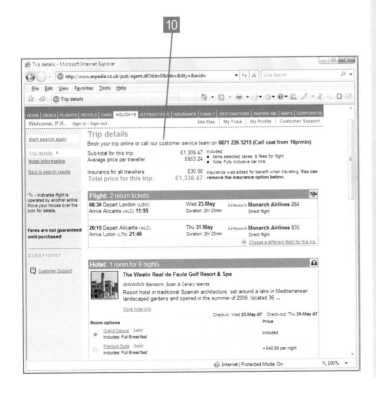

6 Scroll through the list to find the most suitable, then click Choose this flight.

7 Go back to your trip details. If you need to change the car options, do so now.

8 Scroll to the bottom of the page and click Continue booking this trip.

9 You will be offered airport parking. Take it up if needed, then move on.

10 Check the trip details, then continue through to the final booking stage.

11 You will have to register, then give details of the passengers and drivers, and finally, pay for the trip.

## Important

You may be able to get a better deal by booking the flight, car and/or hotel directly. It is always worth checking before you commit yourself.

# Getting an insurance quote

If you want a mortgage, pension, ISA or insurance, check out the web. All significant companies now run sites where you can, at the very least, read about their services. At most, you can get instant quotes or calculations based on your figures. While you should not rush into long-term financial commitments, it's good to be able to get high-quality information online – and it takes very little time.

Direct Line is one of many insurance companies that do most of their business online. The process of getting a quote at their site is simpler and quicker than at some online insurance companies.

## Get an insurance quote from Direct Line

1 Go to Direct Line at www.directline.com.

2 Click the Car Quote link.

3 You will be asked for details of yourself and of your car. For the address, it only needs the postcode and house number, and for the car, it only needs the registration number – there's a link to the DVLA database that tells them the type, model and age.

4 Click **CONTINUE**.

5 If you want to take up the insurance, you can carry on and pay for it online.

**Timesaver tip**

Other major online insurance firms include:

www.churchill.com

www.esure.com

www.admiral.com

www.norwichunion.com.

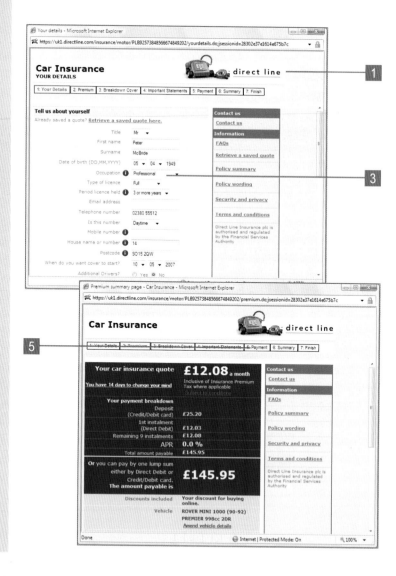

Confused is to insurance what Kelkoo is to shopping. Give your details once to Confused, and they will hunt round the insurers for you and bring you back all the quotes.

It takes a lot longer to enter your details at Confused than at Direct Line, mainly because they are collecting data for a whole bank of insurers, but it's far quicker than going round a load of sites, entering the same details time and again. My test run here produced twenty-five quotes in total – most within 2 minutes – and the cheapest was almost exactly half of the dearest!

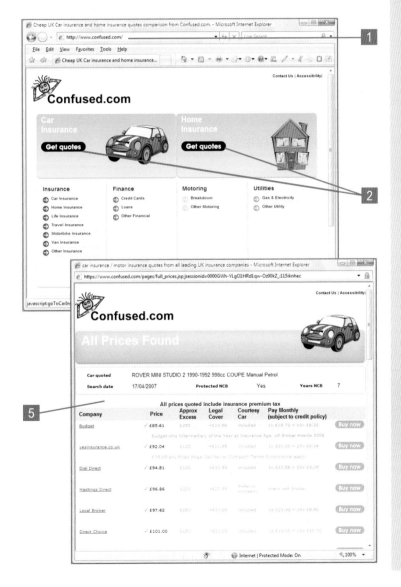

## Getting lots of quotes!

7

1. Go to Confused at www.confused.com.

2. Click the Car Insurance or Home Insurance button.

3. Work through the screens, giving the details of you, any other drivers, and the car.

4. Confused will take your details and start to circulate them. If you wait 2 minutes, it will give you feedback from the fastest sites. If you don't want to wait, click the Exit button.

5. An hour or so later you will get an email with a link to a page at the site where you will be able to see all the quotes.

# Connecting to 50 Connect

50 Connect is a site worth exploring. It offers articles across a wide range of topics, and some carefully selected links to other websites – the One Stop Guide links on the top page are a handy set. The articles and links are organised through channels.

Most parts of the site can be freely visited; some are restricted to members, but membership is free.

**1** Go to 50 Connect at www.50connect.co.uk.

**2** Select a topic in the list of Channels on the left.

**3** Click on a link at the top of the page to go to a select site.

or

**4** Click on a picture, headline or link below to read an article.

Silver Surfers is a directory designed for us older surfers, but recognising that we have the same wide range of interests as younger ones – plus a few more. So, you will find links to age-specific sites, but these are only a small part of the directory.

You won't find as many links here as you will at Yahoo!, but they have been selected more carefully, both for quality and for the intended audience. And look out for the A-Z index – that can be the quickest way to find what you want.

1 Go to Silver Surfers at www.silversurfers.net.

2 Click on a topic heading to go to that page of the directory.

3 Follow the links.

7

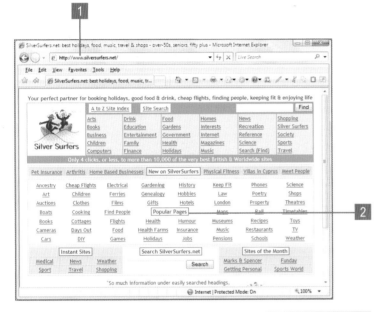

# Surfing with Silver Surfers (cont.)

## Use the index

**4** Click the A–Z Site Index button.

**5** Select a topic.

**6** Follow the links!

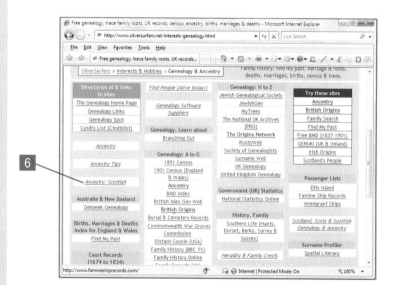

Digital Unite is the new name for Hairnet, the leading IT training organisation for the over 50s. They have a network of trainers – most of them in the same age group – throughout the UK, who give one-to-one training. If you feel that there are aspects of computing that you need help with, you might want to set up a few tailor-made sessions with your local DU trainer.

1 Go to Hairnet at www.hairnet.org.

2 Click the Digital Unite Trainers link.

3 Click the link to Find a trainer near you.

4 Click on the map or the area names to get a list of your local trainers.

5 Pick up their contact details and phone or email them directly.

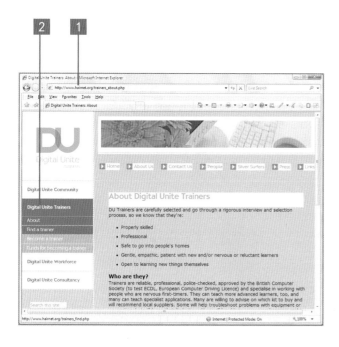

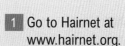

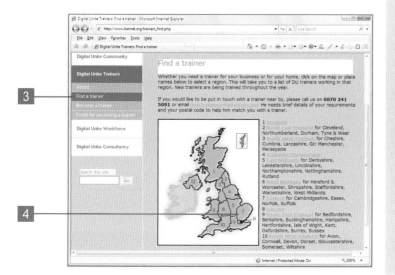

**Important**

I'm not employed by Digital Unite, nor related to them, but I do know them personally, and they do have excellent credentials!

# Getting Skype

Skype is a web-based communications service that enables you to chat (text-talk) to other people in real time, or to talk to them, either through their PCs or normal phones. If you and your contact both have headsets (or microphones and speakers) on your PC and Skype is installed, then you can talk for free – no upfront charges, ho hidden charges! If the other person does not have Skype or the necessary equipment, you can still use your Skype setup to call them on their normal phone. This is charged at a little more than the normal local phone rate – but you could be calling Australia!

If you have distant friends or relations, look closely at Skype. A headset offers the most convenient way to speak and listen, but you can make do with a microphone and speakers. They should simply plug in and work, but if necessary, open the Control Panel and use the Manage Audio Devices routine to set them up.

If you do not have, or do not want, audio, Skype is still an excellent way to communicate with people in real time.

## To install Skype

1 Go to the Skype website at www.skype.com and follow the link to the Download page.

2 Make sure that you have the right version for your PC, then click Download now.

3 Save the file in your Downloads folder or on the Desktop – where you can find it easily later.

4 Once it is downloaded, run the installation file and follow the instructions to install the software – it is very straightforward. As part of the installation, you will need to go online to Skype to join up as a Skype user. There is no charge for this, but if you intend to use the phone facility, you will need to buy some credit at some point.

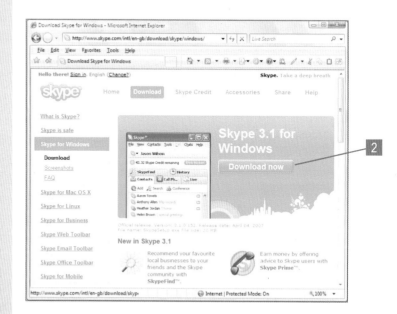

Once you have Skype running, you will soon see what it can do. Explore the tabs and the menus.

■ Contacts will list your contacts, once you start adding them. Initially there will only be the testing centre link.

■ Call Phones is used for making calls to standard landline or mobile phones.

■ Live lists public conversations – conference calls that you can join in on. At the time of writing, these have yet to become really popular.

■ History gives you a summary of your recent chats and calls.

■ Skypefind is where Skype users let each other know about good shops, services, bars and restaurants. You can recommend your favourites here, and find ones recommended by other people. It's a kind of very selective Yellow Pages.

## Discovering Skype's features

1 Run Skype, from the Start menu or Desktop.

2 Click on each of the tabs to see what's there.

3 Click back on the Contacts tab.

4 If you want to use the phone facilities, select Skype Test Call and click ◔. Once you are through, you should be invited to record a message. Speak! If you can hear your recorded message, you will know that your Skypephone is ready for use.

7

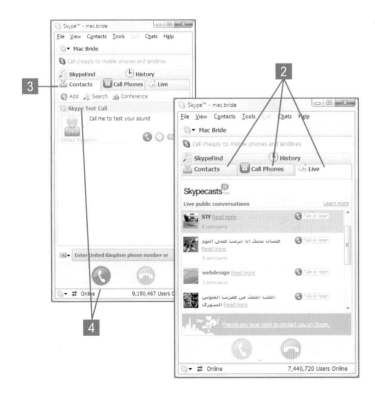

# Adding a Skype contact

If you want to call someone on the phone, all you need is their number. If you want to call them on their PC or chat to them, then you need to add them to your contacts list. This is a two-way, two-stage process. First, you alert them that you would like to add them to your contacts, then they return the connection to complete. People do not have to agree to be in your contacts.

Skype can be intrusive – people can start chatting to you while you are trying to do other things. And people can get upset if you don't reply. So, let your contacts know if you are busy or if you are going away from your desk.

1  Click the Add button on the Contacts tab.

2  Type in the person's Skype name (if you know it), or otherwise their full name or email address.

3  Click [ Find ].

4  If you are searching by name, there may be several possibilities. If you are searching by email address or Skype name, there should be only one. Select the person and click [ Add Skype Contact ].

5  At the 'Say hello' dialogue box, add a message to introduce yourself.

6  Click [ OK ].

7  Wait. If the person is online, you may get a reply almost immediately.

## To change your Skype status

8  Click the Status icon at the bottom left of the Skype window.

9  Select the appropriate setting.

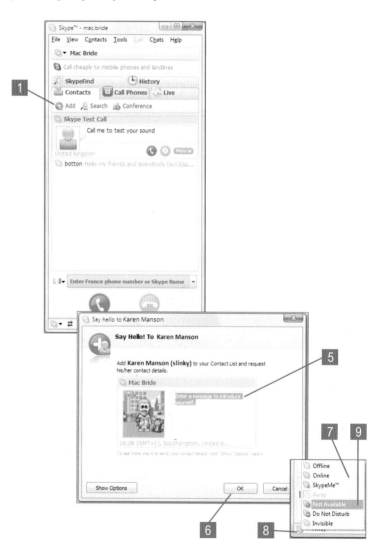

How you make a call depends on whether or not you are calling to another Skype user, or a normal phone line. You start on the Contacts tab when calling another Skype user, but otherwise on the Call Phones tab.

Make sure that your headset is plugged in and ready before you start!

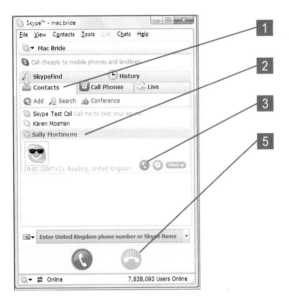

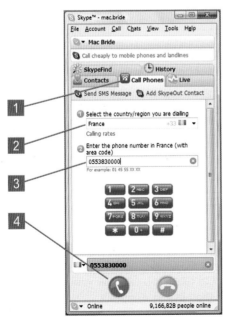

## Making a Skype phone call

### To call a Skype contact

1 Switch to the Contacts tab.

2 Click on the person's name.

3 Click the 🕓 icon by their name or at the bottom of the window.

4 Wait for them to answer. Enjoy your conversation!

5 When you are finished, click the 🔴 icon.

### To call a normal phone

1 Switch to the Call Phones tab.

2 Select the country to dial.

3 Type in the phone number, or use the on-screen number pad to dial.

4 Click the 🕓 icon, and carry on as for a Skype call.

### Timesaver tip

If you call someone regularly, add them as a SkypeOut contact. This stores their name and number, and lists them on the Contacts tab. You can then start a dial-out call from there with a single click.

# Chatting by Skype ▶

1. On the Contacts tab, select the person and click the ⊙ icon.

2. Type your message. Press [Enter] to send the finished message. If the other person is online, and has the time (and the inclination) they will write back.

3. Keep on typing and reading.

4. If you want to send an 'emoticon' – an animated picture – click on the Emoticons button to open the palette, and click on the one you want.

5. That's about it. There's no actual signing-off routine. You should say 'goodbye' when you've finished, but that's just simple courtesy.

In Internet slang, 'chatting' is done with the hands, not the voicebox. It is typed, two-way, communication – and it's instantaneous as long as the connections are working properly. It can take a little getting used to. The main thing to note is this: although it is two-way and in real time, you cannot tell when someone is in the middle of writing to you, and there is no rule that says you can only send one message each in turn. The result is that you may well find that while you are typing a response, a second – or third – message comes in from the other person (they may type faster than you, or be sending shorter messages) and the chat gets out of synch. It can lead to misunderstandings...

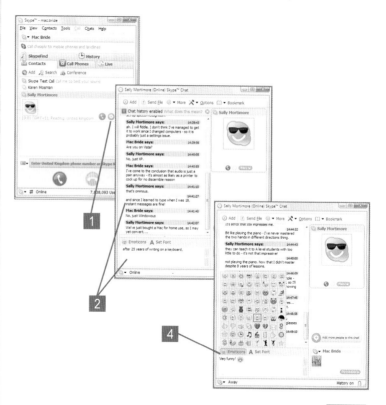

## ? Did you know?

If you have a web cam, the other person can see you as you chat. The quality is not very good – it's jerky and low resolution, but at least you can see your kids regularly – even if they live in Australia.

Your Skype profile carries basic information about you that you are happy for your contacts, or other Skype users, to see – your Skype name, location, language, local time and the number of your contacts. It can also have a picture of you – a photo from your own files, or you can create a cartoon image.

While you are editing your profile, you might also like to check and change your Skype settings.

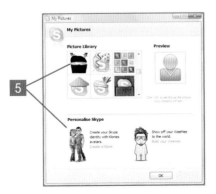

1 Open the Tools menu and select Options.

2 Check the General options, and change any to suit. You can come back to these at any time if you find the settings don't work quite how you'd like.

3 Click Edit my Skype Profile.

4 Information in the top section will be visible to any Skype users who come across your name. Put in as much or as little as you want to make public.

5 Details in the bottom left are visible to your contacts. Click Change to choose a picture from your own files, or to create a Klonie or a WeeMe – cartoon characters to represent you. (Have fun playing with these!)

6 Add your email address to the private details if you want people who know that address to be able to find you on Skype. (The address is not published by Skype.)

# Sending files by Skype

You can send files through Skype, then chat about them with your contact.

1 On the Contacts tab, locate the person you want to send the file to. It helps if you let them know the file is coming – but this is not essential.

2 Click the Menu button and select Send File.

3 A standard Open dialogue box will appear. Locate the file and click Open .

4 The Sending file window will open. Nothing will happen until the recipient agrees to accept the file. If no one is there, you will have to wait.

5 When the file is sent, it will travel fairly slowly (at least, it will appear slow if you are used to downloading files at broadband speeds).

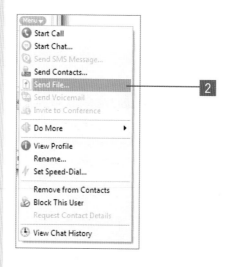

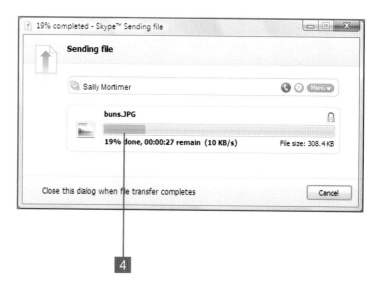

## Did you know?

The Conference Call facility allows you to talk to several people at once, and it can be a combination of Skype calls and calls to actual phones.

# Windows Mail

## Introduction

There are quite a few email programs around, but Windows Mail is used far more than others. There are two reasons for its popularity: it's simple and efficient to use; and – the main reason – it is the software that comes with Windows, along with Internet Explorer, so it's probably in your machine already.

If you are one of those rare people with a different email program, don't stop reading. Almost all email software works in virtually the same way as Windows Mail. Commands may be arranged on menus and toolbars in different orders, but they will still give you the same range of facilities. New messages are read and written in the same way; old messages are managed in the same way and can be stored in a similar system of folders; there are the same kind of options.

A few minutes is all it normally takes to find your way round an email screen. The key things to remember are that the Inbox is where new messages arrive, that they will remain there until you delete them or move them to another folder; and that the Outbox is where your outgoing messages are stored if you write them when you are offline.

## What you'll do

**Explore Windows Mail**

**Explore the toolbar**

**Pick up your mail**

**Add an address to Windows Contacts**

**Edit a Contacts entry**

**Sort your Contacts**

**Find a contact**

**Create an email group**

**Write a message**

**Format, customise and spell-check a message**

**Reply to an email**

**Forward a message**

**Organise your old mail**

**Find messages**

**Attach a file to a message**

**Save and open an attached file**

**Set up a Yahoo! mail account**

**Read and send messages at Yahoo! mail**

# Exploring
# Windows Mail

In Chapter 1 you met the three key elements of the Windows Mail window: the Folder list, the Headers pane and the Preview pane. There are another six elements that can be included in the display. Apart from the Headers pane, every element is optional and can be easily switched off if you decide that you do not want it.

Mail bar          Folder bar          Views bar

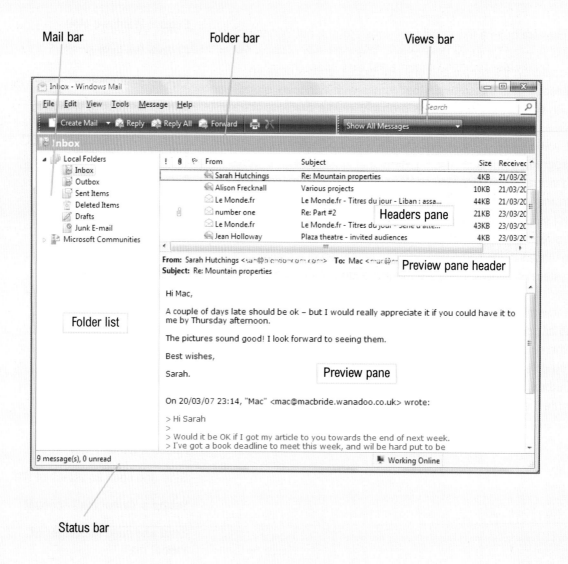

Status bar

- The **Views bar** lets you switch between displaying all messages and those you have not yet read. The options are also available on the **View** menu.

- The **Folder bar** shows the name of the current folder.

- The **Folder list** shows your email and news folders. New email folders can be created if needed, and newsgroup folders are created automatically when you subscribe to groups. The contents of the current folder are displayed in the Headers area.

- The **Headers pane** is the only part of the display which is not optional, but even here you can control the layout and which items are displayed.

- The **Preview pane** displays the current message from the Headers area. If this pane is turned off, messages are displayed in a new window. The pane can sit below or beside the Headers – below is usually more convenient.

- The **Preview pane header** repeats the From and Subject details from the Headers area.

- The **Status bar**, as always, helps to keep you informed of what's going on. Amongst other things, it tells you how many messages are in a folder, and shows the addresses behind hyperlinks in emails.

8

See also

Controlling the Preview pane, page 215.
Changing the Headers pane, page 217.

# Exploring the toolbar

Create Mail  Reply  Reply All  Forward  Print  Delete  Send/Receive  Contacts  Find  Folder list

Windows Mail has a lot of commands that most of us will rarely use, and if you don't join the newsgroups (see Chapter 10), there are some that you will never use at all. In practice, all the commands that you will use regularly can be found on buttons on the toolbar.

## Create Mail
Click the button to start a new message in plain text or with the default formatting, or click the arrow to open a drop-down list and select your Stationery (see page 199).

## Reply
Starts a new message to the sender of the current message – the same as Reply to Sender on the Message menu.

## Reply All
Sends a reply to all the people who had copies of the message – the same as Message, Reply to All.

## Forward
Copies the message into the New Message window, ready for you to send it on to another person, adding your own comments if you like. The same as Message, Forward.

## Print
Prints the current message, using the default printer settings.

## Delete
Deletion is a two-stage process. Clicking this button transfers the selected message(s) to the Deleted Items folder. Messages are then deleted

from there when you close Windows Mail – if this option is turned on (see page 228) – or when you delete them from the Deleted Items folder.

## Send/Receive
Sends anything sitting in the Outbox and picks up any new mail. If there's something in your Outbox that you do not want to send yet, e.g. a message with a big attachment that will take a long time to send, open the Tools menu and use Receive All instead.

Similarly, if you are in a hurry to send a message but do not have time to deal with incoming mail, you can use Tools, Send All.

## Contacts
Opens your Windows Contacts, to add a new contact, or to manage existing ones.

## Find
Will search through your stored messages, on the basis of the sender, subject, text within the message, date or other factors. This is the same as Find on the Edit menu (see page 192).

## Folder List
Toggles the Folder List on and off.

> ### See also
>
> You can change the selection of buttons in the toolbar, and tweak its appearance. See Customising the toolbar, page 216.

Unlike snail mail, email does not get delivered directly to you. Instead, it goes into a mailbox at the provider and you must go online to get it. You can set Windows Mail to check for new mail automatically on start-up and/or at regular intervals while you are online, or you can pick up your mail when you feel like it.

New mail is placed into the Inbox folder. If this is selected, its sender, subject, date and other details will be listed, in bold, in the Headers area. Select a message to read it.

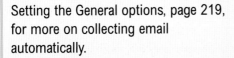

See also

Setting the General options, page 219, for more on collecting email automatically.

## Picking up your mail

1 If you are not online already, get connected now.

2 Click the Send/Receive button drop-down arrow then select Receive All or open the Tools menu, point to Send and Receive and select Send and Receive All.

3 Wait while the messages come in.

4 Click once on a message in the Headers pane to open it in the Preview pane.

5 If the message is clearly junk, delete it immediately.

6 Read the message, then:

Delete it

Reply to it

Forward it to someone else

Print it

Save it, or

Move it to another folder for long term storage.

8

# Adding an address to Windows Contacts

Windows Contacts isn't just a convenience, it is an essential tool for email. Addresses are rarely easy to remember and if you get just one letter wrong, the message won't get through. But if an address is stored in your Contacts, you can pick it from there whenever you need it.

Addresses can be added in two ways: you can type them in directly, or if you are replying to people who have written to you, you can get Windows Mail to copy their addresses into Contacts.

1 Click the  button or open the Tools menu and select Windows Contacts.

2 When the address list opens, click New Contact.

3 Type in the person's name, splitting it into First, Middle and Last – the separate parts can be used for sorting the list. You can miss out any you don't need, or put the whole name into one slot.

4 Add a brief Nickname if you like – this can be used for selecting addresses later.

5 Type the address in the Email addresses slot, then click Add .

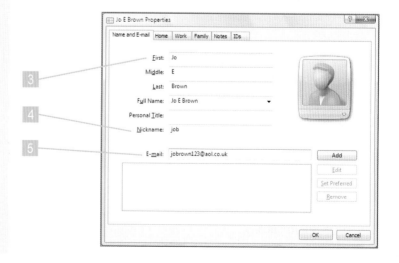

Contacts can store more than just email addresses. You can also add other contact information – home and business addresses and phone numbers – whatever is relevant; there is also space for the names of your contact's spouse and children, and even their birthday and anniversary dates. How much you put here is entirely up to you.

6 Switch to the Home or Work tab if you want to store the snail mail address or phone number.

7 Switch to the Family tab if you want to add family details or dates to remember.

8 Click [ OK ].

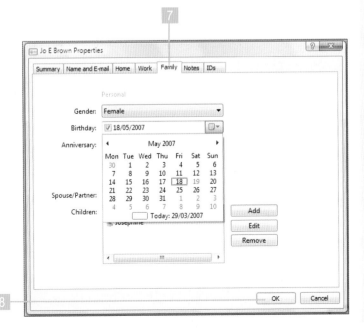

# Editing a
# Contacts entry

Details change – people move, they change their Internet service provider, and therefore their email address, and phone numbers seem to be reorganised every few years. If you need to change or add details to an existing entry, it is easily done.

If a contact's new address has been copied into Contacts when you replied to them, it will have created a new entry. If the old entry only contains the email address, then it is probably simpler to delete that and use the new entry.

## Edit an entry

1. Select the contact in the list.

2. Click on the person's picture or icon in the right-hand pane.

3. Edit the entry as required.

## Delete an entry

4. Select the contact in the list.

5. Right-click and select Delete.

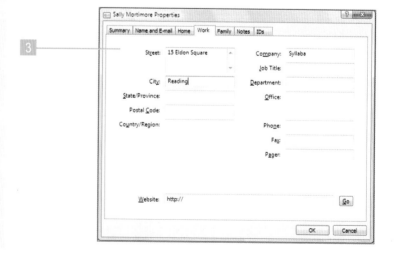

The entries in Contacts are normally held in alphabetical order of the whole name, so 'John Smith' comes after 'Jane Smith', but before 'William Brown'.

You can sort into ascending or descending order of any column, by clicking on the heading. And Windows Contacts is, of course, just a folder in Explorer, so you can sort, group or filter the entries here, as you can any other files.

# Sorting your Contacts

1 Click on the heading of any column to sort into ascending order of that column.

or

2 Click twice on a heading to sort into descending order.

or

3 Open the View menu, point to Sort By and select a property.

4 If you want to change the order, repeat View, Sort By and select the order.

8

# Finding a contact

If there are only a couple of dozen entries in your Contacts, you should be able to find a person simply by scrolling through the list. As the numbers rise, it can take longer to spot the entry that you need. Searching is the answer.

If you type a few letters of the name into the Search box, Contacts will filter the list to display only those that match. The more of the name that you type, the more the displayed set will shrink.

1 If Contacts is not active, open the Tools menu and select Windows Contacts.

2 Type the first few letters – or any part of the name – into the Search box at the top right of the window.

3 Check the display as it is filtered, to see if the entry has been found.

4 Type more of the name if necessary.

## Timesaver tip

Sometimes, email addresses will go into the Contacts list without their matching real names. If the email address bears no resemblance to their real name – and it happens – then the search will be more difficult. Try to remember something of the address, or of the company that the person works for, and search on that.

When you write a message, you can send it to any number of people, just by adding all their names to the To: box. If you regularly write to the same set of people, there is a simpler way of doing this. You can create a group in Contacts, and use this instead of individual addresses when writing the email.

A group can be created quickly if the member's details are already in Contacts. If you do not have a member's details, they can be typed in directly.

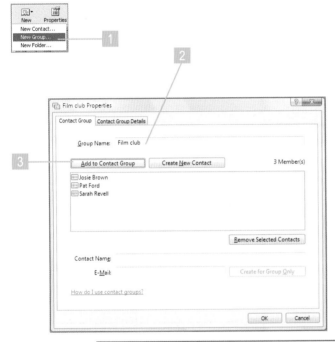

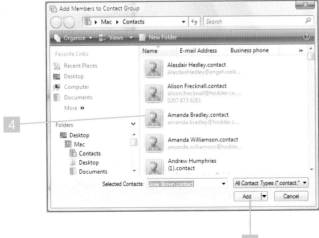

1. Click the New button and select New Group...
2. Type a name for the group.
3. Click Add to Contact Group.
4. Select contact – hold down [Ctrl] if you want to select more than one at a time.
5. Click Add ▼.

8

# Creating an email group (cont.)

**6** Back at the group's properties dialogue box, if you want to add someone who is not in your Contacts, enter their name and email and click Create for Group Only .

**7** If you want to store a street address, phone number of other information for the group, switch to the Group Details tab and enter it there.

**8** Click OK .

**Important**

People added into a group in this way will not have an entry in Contacts. If you want them in your Contacts, click the Create New Contact button and start from there.

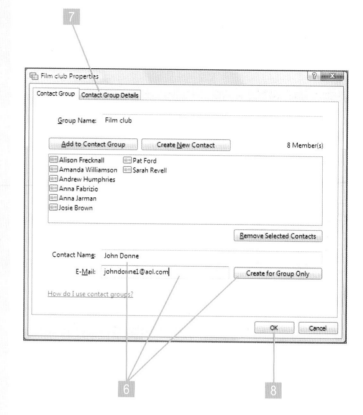

**7**

Film club Properties

Contact Group | Contact Group Details

Group Name: Film club

Add to Contact Group | Create New Contact | 8 Member(s)

Alison Frecknall | Pat Ford
Amanda Williamson | Sarah Revell
Andrew Humphries
Anna Fabrizio
Anna Jarman
Josie Brown

Remove Selected Contacts

Contact Name: John Donne

E-Mail: johndonne1@aol.com | Create for Group Only

How do I use contact groups?

OK | Cancel

**6**

**8**

Messages are written in the New Message window. The main part of this is the writing area, but in the top part of the window there are several boxes which must be attended to.

- To: is the address of the recipient(s).

- Cc: (carbon copy) is for the addresses of those people, if any, to whom you want to send copies.

- You can also have Bcc: (blind carbon copy) recipients if you select their names from your Address Book. These people will not be listed, as the To and Cc recipients will be, at the top of the message.

- Subject: a few words outlining the nature of your message, so that your recipients know what's coming.

1. Open the File menu, point to New and select Mail Message or click Create Mail.

2. Click To: to open your Contacts.

3. Select a contact and click To: ->, Cc: -> or Bcc: ->, to copy the name into a recipient box.

   Repeat Step 3 if you want to add more recipients.

4. Click OK to return to the New Message window.

5. Enter a Subject for the message.

6. Type the message.

8

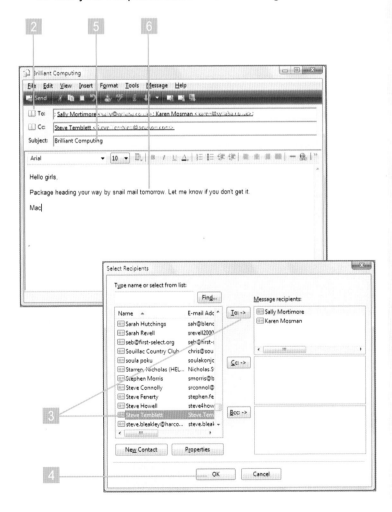

# Writing a message (cont.)

A message can be sent immediately after it has been written, or stored in the Outbox to be sent later. If you have a broadband connection, you would normally be online while you are writing the messages, and would send messages immediately. If you connect through the normal phone line, being online ties up the phone and (probably) costs money. In this case, you would be better to write your messages offline, store them in the Outbox then send all the new ones in one batch.

You can set the options so that either the Send button will send immediately or it will store messages. If you want to handle a message differently, there are Send and Send Later commands.

7 Click  to use the default Send option.

or

8 Open the File menu and select Send Message or Send Later.

9 When you have finished all your writing, if there are messages in the Outbox, click 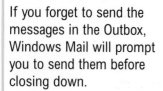. If you aren't online, the Connect dialogue box will appear, ready to connect to your ISP.

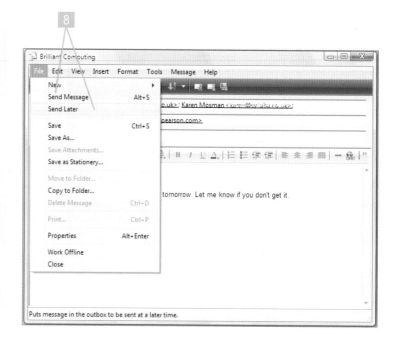

## Timesaver tip

If you forget to send the messages in the Outbox, Windows Mail will prompt you to send them before closing down.

An email message can have plain or formatted text. The formatting, which is done with HTML, offers the normal range of fonts, size, style, colour and alignment options. You can write hyperlinks into a message, so that the reader can go straight to a web page. You can also insert images, or text from other documents.

To send formatted messages, the New Message window must be in Rich Text (HTML) mode – if it is, the Formatting toolbar will be present. If you didn't set HTML as the default in the options (see page 222), you can switch to it before writing the message.

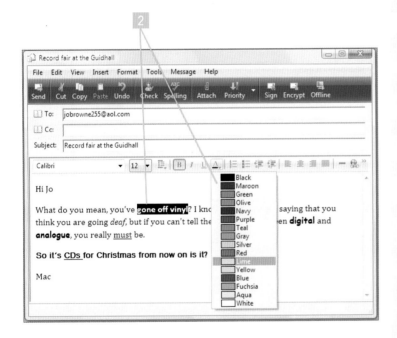

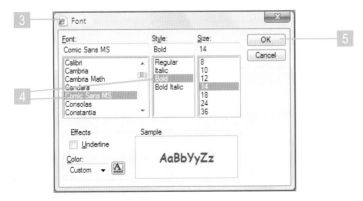

1 If you can't see the Formatting toolbar, open the Format menu and select Rich Text (HTML).

2 To format text, select it and use the toolbar buttons.

or

3 Open the Format menu, select Font... to open the Font dialogue box

4 Define the font style, size and colour.

5 Click ⬚ OK ⬚.

**8**

### Timesaver tip

Don't feel obliged to spend time formatting a message. Very few people bother to format their email – this is a quick and casual form of communication.

# Defining the background

As well as formatting the text of the message, you can also define the background, setting it as a plain colour or a picture.

Windows Mail comes with a small set of pictures, some of which are for use as backgrounds. The others are dividing lines or banners to brighten up the top. Don't get them confused – the dividers make terrible backgrounds!

1 Open the Format menu, point to Background, then Colour and pick a colour from the list.

or

2 Open the Format menu, point to Background and select Picture…

3 Click Browse….

4 At the file selection dialogue box, click the View button and select Thumbnails – it helps if you can see the pictures.

5 Select a suitable picture.

6 Click Open.

7 Click OK.

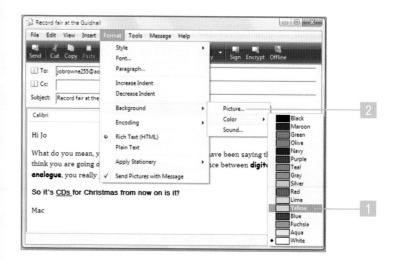

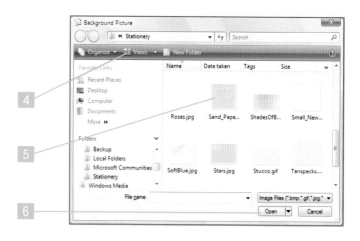

## Did you know?

You can use any suitable picture as a background. It must be in GIF format.

Stationery gives a coordinated text colour and background to a message. You can start a new message using stationery or apply it to an existing message.

# Using stationery

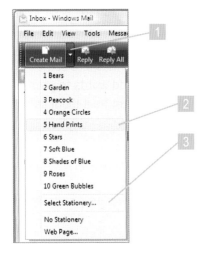

## Start with stationery

1. Click the arrow beside the Create Mail button.

2. Select a stationery style from the drop-down list.

or

3. Click on Select Stationery…

4. Pick a style from the Select Stationery dialogue box.

## Apply stationery to a message

5. Open the Format menu, point to Apply Stationery and pick a style.

or

6. Click on More Stationery… to pick from the dialogue box.

**Important**

If the stationery includes a banner or dividing line, this will not be included if you apply the style to an existing message.

## Spell-checking a message

Even though email is generally treated as a casual form of communication, spell-checking is still worthwhile – some mistypes can be causes of great confusion!

You can opt for automatic spell checking, or run the spell checker when you are ready.

Windows Mail has a good dictionary, but names and some technical terms may be missing. You can add words to your own dictionary so that spell checker does not treat them as errors the next time around.

 If automatic spell-checking is turned on, the check will start when you click ![Send].

otherwise

2 Click ![Spelling].

3 When the checker meets a word it does not recognise, it will ask you what to do.

4 Click [Ignore] to leave it as you wrote it, or [Ignore All] if the word occurs several times.

5 Pick a word from the Suggestions list and click [Change] to replace it, or [Change All] if there are several occurrences.

6 Click [Add] to add it to your own dictionary.

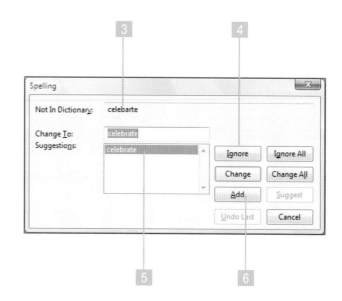

See also

See Setting the Spelling options, on page 225 for more on controlling the spell checker.

Replying to someone else's email is the simplest and most reliable way to send a message, because the address is already there for you.

When you start to reply, the original text may be copied into your message. You can decide whether or not this should happen, and how the copied text is to be displayed – and you will see how to do this in Chapter 9. For the moment, go with the default settings.

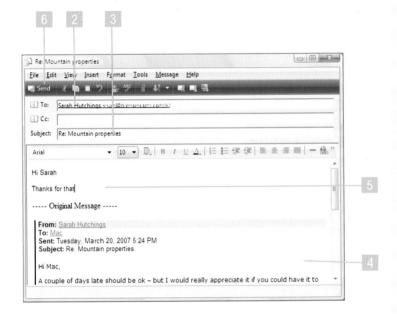

1 When you click  the Compose window will open.

2 The To: field will already have the email address in it – though it may actually display the person's name. Don't worry about that.

3 The Subject: field will have the original Subject text, preceded by 'Re:'. Edit this if you like.

4 The message area may have the original text copied in. You can edit or delete this if you like.

5 Add your own message.

6 Click .

**See also**

See Setting the Send options, on page 222, for more on copying the text in a reply.

# Forwarding a message

If someone sends you a message that you would like to share with other people, you can do this easily by forwarding. The subject and message are copied into the New Message window, so all you have to do is add the address of the recipients and any comments of your own.

1. Select the message and click **Forward**.

2. Add the To: address and any comments of your own.

3. Trim out any unwanted material from the original.

4. Click **Send**.

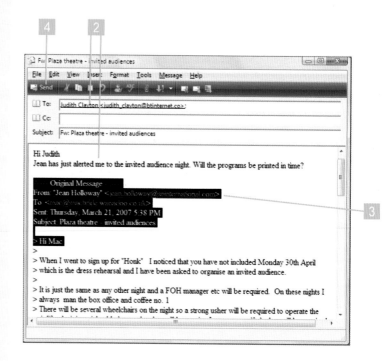

Email can clog up your system. This is partly because you tend to get more than you want, but mainly because most of us leave messages in the Inbox after reading. Think about what we do with paper letters. After reading them, we normally either bin them, or file them, or put them on one side until we have dealt with them and then bin or file them. Why don't we do the same with email?

I think it's because old messages don't visibly clutter up your desk – but they are still clutter! Tidying up your Inbox takes little time, saves hard disk space and makes it easier to find those old messages that you did want to keep.

Create one or more folders for long-term storage using the File, New Folder command, then go through your old messages, deleting them or moving them to appropriate folders.

◀ **Organising your old mail**

1 On the File menu, point to New and select Folder…

2 Enter a meaningful name for the folder.

3 Pick the folder within which it is to go – select Inbox to put it at the top level.

4 Click OK .

5 Open the Inbox.

6 To move a message, select it, drag it across the window and drop it into the target folder.

7 To delete a message, select it and press the [Delete] key or click Delete .

8

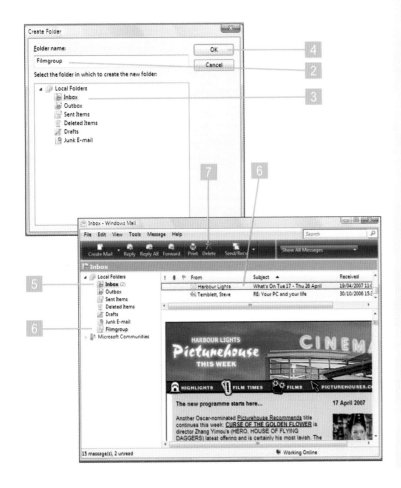

# Finding a message

Unless you are very organised (or keep very little old mail), there will be times when you can't lay your hands on a particular message. When this happens, try the Find routine. This can search through your messages to locate ones that match any given criteria. At the simplest, you could search through one folder to find a message that had a certain word in its text.

1 Use the Folder List to switch to the folder containing the message.

2 Click ▣ or open the Edit menu, point to Find and select Message... The Find Message window will open.

3 In the Message field, type one or more words that you know will be in the text of the missing message.

4 Click Find Now and wait a moment.

5 Matching messages will be listed at the bottom of the window. Double-click the messages to open them.

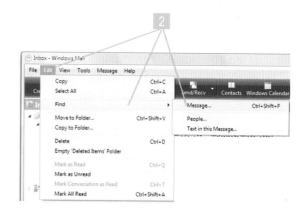

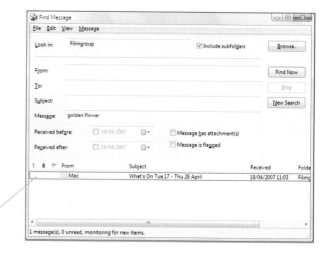

Matching text is not the only way to find a message. You can search on the basis of who it was received from or sent to, the subject, the date, and whether or not it had an attachment or was flagged.

To set a date, click the arrow to the right of the date field to display a calendar. Use the arrows at the top to change the month, and pick a date by clicking on the number.

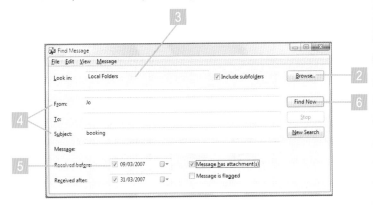

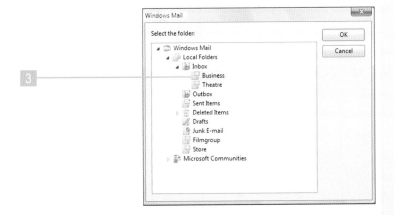

1 Open the Find Message window, as before.

2 If you need to change to a different folder, click Browse... .

3 Select the folder to search – if you want to search all the folders, select Local Folders – then click OK .

4 If you know, enter all or part of the name of the person it was From, or something from the Subject line, or the main text.

5 If you know roughly when the message arrived, set the dates that it was received before or after.

6 Click Find Now , and read the matching message, as before.

8

## Attaching a file to a message

Images, documents, music, programs and other non-text files can be sent by mail, attached to messages. As the mail system was designed for transmitting plain text, other files have to be converted to text for transfer, and back to binary on receipt. Windows Mail handles these conversions for you, but you need to be aware of the conversion, because it increases the size of file by about 50%. Big files get even bigger.

1 Start a new message as usual.

2 Open the Insert menu and select File Attachment... or click.

3 The Insert Attachment dialogue box is essentially the same as the Open File dialogue box. If you are looking for a picture, it may help if you switch to Thumbnails view.

4 Locate and select the file, then click Open.

5 The file will be listed in a new Attach slot beneath the Subject line. Complete the message.

6 Click Send and wait – it takes a few moments for the system to convert the file.

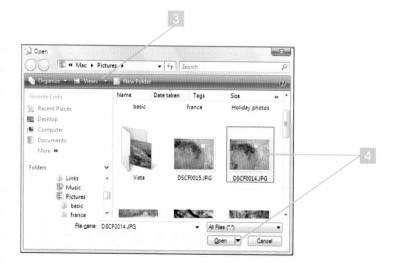

### Important

If you have a dial-up connection, very large attached files can be a problem. If the connection is broken during transmission, you have to start sending or receiving again from scratch, and messages are sent in the order in which they are created or arrive in your mailbox – so a big file will block your communications until it gets through. And remember that this also applies to the people to whom you are sending messages – don't send people big files unless they want them!

You'll know if an incoming message has an attachment as there will be a little paperclip icon 🔗 beside it in the header list. If you have opted to show the preview pane header, you will also find a larger clip icon there.

For this next exercise you need a message with an attached file. So, you can either wait until someone sends you one, or you can attach a file to a message, set it to send later – so that it is in the Outbox – and then open the message. (And don't forget to delete it later if you only created the message to test the procedure!).

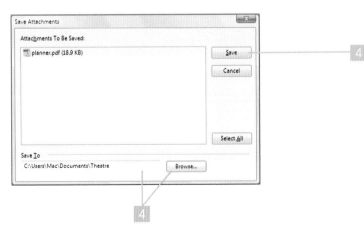

1 Open the message.

2 If the preview pane header is present, click the paperclip icon 🔗 and select Save Attachments...

otherwise

3 Open the File menu and select Save Attachments...

4 Locate the folder in which to store the file, then click Save.

**8**

### Timesaver tip

If a picture has been attached to an HTML-formatted message, you will be able to see it. Right-click on it and select the Save Picture As... command – it's exactly the same technique as you would use for capturing an image of a web page.

# Opening an attachment

Open the message.

If the preview pane header is present, click the paperclip icon  and select the name of the attachment.

otherwise

Double-click on the message to open it in its own window, then right-click on the filename in the Attach line and select Open.

At the Mail Attachment dialogue box, think again and if you have any doubts about the file's safety, click Cancel.

If you are confident that it is safe, click Open.

You can open an attachment directly from a message, without saving it. But take care. Some very nasty viruses are spread through email attachments. You get a message, apparently from an acquaintance, and when you open it, the virus program is executed. Typically, it will go through your address book, sending virus-laden messages to your contacts, and it may also destroy the files on the hard drive.

Any executable file (program) may be a virus. Common extensions for executable files include: .exe, .com, .bat, .vbx. Viruses can also be hidden in macros – programs that run within applications. These can be a problem in Word, Excel and PowerPoint. If you have any of these, make sure that they are set for high security in respect of macros. Go to the Tools menu, point to Macros, select Security... and set the level to High.

Go to almost any of the major directories and portals and you will be offered free web mail. This is much the same as ordinary email but with two big differences.

The first is that you can handle your web mail from anywhere as long as you can log on to the Internet somehow. This may be through a public terminal in a library or Internet cafe, from a friend's desktop, or wherever.

The second is that you can (normally) only use web mail online. Your messages are stored online and you must be online while you are dealing with your mail (though you can download messages for later reading, and upload messages written in a word-processor).

A web mail address is worth considering if you are often away from home, either on holiday or staying with friends or family.

The example here is from Yahoo! mail. Other major web mail providers include Hotmail, Excite and Google.

1. In Internet Explorer, go to uk.yahoo.com and click Sign up, then click Get Yahoo! Mail.

2. Enter your name, password and other details. You will be asked to give a user name. Your first choice of name may already be in use, but there's no harm in trying. Click Check Availability of This ID . You may need to come up with a new name or a variation on it.

3. Give a little more information for security purposes – you need to be able to prove who you are if you forget your password!

4. Accept the terms, and you are signed up.

8

# Reading a message at Yahoo! mail

Running an email account online is not really different from running one through Windows Mail, once you have accommodated to the layout, and to the fact of working within the browser. The Inbox is there, and new messages are listed with their sender, subject, date and size showing. When you select a message for reading, it will be opened in the same window.

1 If you are not already there, click the Mail button and select Check Mail to go to your Inbox.

2 Click on the Subject to open the message.

3 Use the buttons to delete, reply to or forward the message.

4 Click on the Inbox link to read any other messages.

## For your information

When you first arrive, there will be a Welcome message from Yahoo! Mail – so there's bound to be something to read!

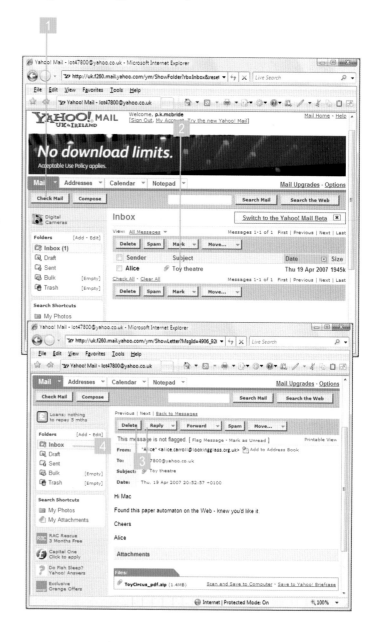

210

Messages are written in the Compose window, in Rich Text (HTML), and can have files – from your PC or elsewhere on the Internet – attached to them, just as they can in Windows Mail.

But before you write a message to anyone, you should add them to your addresses. Addresses are not stored automatically, and there is no simple way to transfer one from your new mail to the address list.

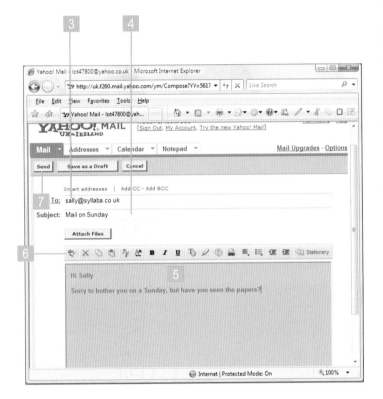

1 Click the Addresses button and check that the name is in the list. If not, add it now.

2 Click the Compose button in the Mail window.

3 Start to type the name in the To field. Any matching names from your addresses will be listed – select the one you want.

4 Enter a Subject.

5 Write and format your message as normal.

6 Click  to spell-check the message.

7 When you are finished, click Send .

8

# Customising Windows Mail

## Introduction

If you find yourself using email a lot, you will want to customise Windows Mail to suit the way you work. There is a great deal of flexibility built into the software so do explore the options and create a work space adapted to your needs.

**9**

# Adjusting the layout

There are several ways in which you can customise your display. The first of these is to select the screen elements that you want to include in the layout. This is done in the Window Layout Properties dialogue box. Simply tick or clear the ticks to turn elements on and off.

1 Open the View menu and select Layout...

2 In the Basic area, click on the check boxes to turn an element on or off.

3 Click [ Apply ] to see the effect of your changes.

4 Go back to step 2 if you don't like the new layout.

5 Click [ OK ] to return to Outlook Express, or leave the dialog box open and read on...

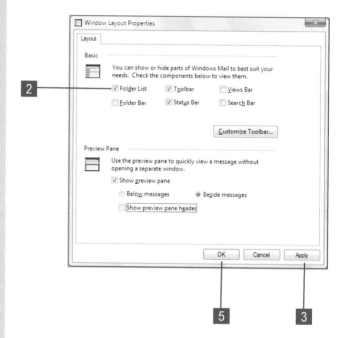

## Important

The only elements that you really need are the Folder List – to move between your folders – and the Toolbar (unless you prefer to work from the menus).

The Preview pane is optional – a message can also be opened into its own window. If the pane is present, it automatically displays whatever message is selected in the Headers pane. This can be useful, but it can also be a cause of problems – it all depends on how good the filters are at your Internet service provider. If they are filtering out the spam and those messages that contain viruses, then the Preview pane can be used safely. If not, turn the pane off so that you control which messages are opened.

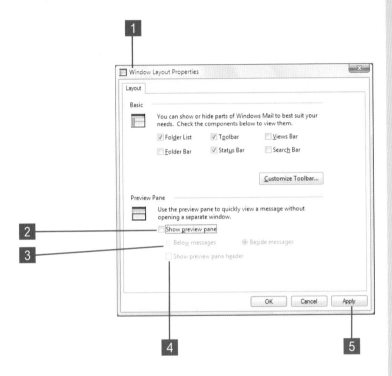

### Controlling the Preview pane

1. Open the View menu and select Layout… to open the Window Layout Properties dialogue box.

2. In the Preview Pane area, click the checkbox to turn the pane on or off.

   If the pane is on…

3. Select where the pane is to go – below is generally better as you can normally read the whole width of the message without scrolling the display.

4. Turn on the preview pane header if you want it – it simply repeats the From and Subject information from the Headers pane.

5. Click OK or Apply.

9

### See also

For more on spam and filtering, see Creating a message rule, page 231.

# Customising the toolbar

As with Internet Explorer (and most other Windows programs) you can adjust the contents and appearance of the toolbar to suit yourself. You can add or remove buttons, set the size of the icons and choose whether to show text labels on all buttons, on a selected few, or on none.

**1** Open the View menu, select Layout... and click
Customize Toolbar...

or

**2** Right-click on the toolbar and select Customise...

**3** To add a button, select it from the left-hand pane and click
Add ->. It will be added above (i.e. to the left) of the selected item in the current list.

**4** To change a button's position, use the Move Up and Move Down buttons.

**5** To remove a button, select it and click Remove.

**6** Click the arrow to the right of the Text options slot and choose how to handle the labels.

**7** Set the size of the icons as required in the Icon options drop-down list.

**8** Click Close when you have finished.

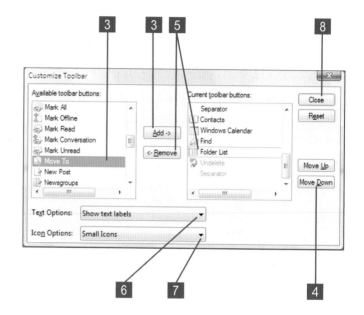

You can change the layout, and the choice, of the columns in the Headers pane, so that you can see the information that you need. The main columns are:

Priority – messages can be marked as high or low priority.

Attachment – indicates that a file is attached to the message (see page 208).

Flag – for you to mark the message.

From – who sent it?

Subject – the contents of the Subject line.

Received – when it arrived in the mailbox at your service provider.

Size – how big is it?

Sent – when it was sent.

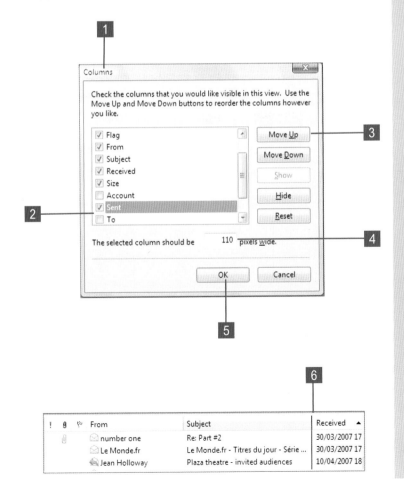

# Changing the Headers pane

**1** Open the View menu and select Columns… to open the Columns dialogue box.

**2** Tick the columns you want to include (click to remove the tick if you don't want them).

**3** To change the position of a column, select it and click Move Up to move it up the list (and left across the display) or Move Down to move it down (and to the right).

**4** You can set the width of the column by entering the size in pixels, but its easier to do this later with the mouse.

**5** Click OK .

**6** Back at the main display, click on the line between the headings and drag to adjust the width of the columns as required.

9

# Sorting the headers

You can change the order of messages so that you can find (old) messages more easily. They can be sorted by the contents of any column and in either ascending or descending order. If you sort by From, for example, the messages will be grouped by sender's name in alphabetical (or reverse) order; sort them by Received and they will be in date order.

1 Click on the label to sort the messages into ascending order of that column.

2 Click again to sort into descending order. (An arrowhead will indicate the direction.)

or

3 Open the View menu, point to Sort By and select the column.

4 Select the sort order.

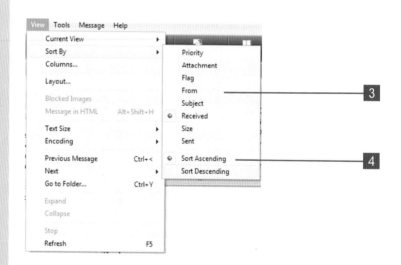

## Timesaver tip

If messages are sorted in Received order, you can easily see when new ones arrive as they will be together at the top (or bottom) of the list.

The General options control what happens when you start Windows Mail, and how you send and receive mail. When setting these, the key questions to ask yourself are:

■ Do you use the newsgroups? If not, turn off Notify me…

■ Do you use Windows Messenger? If not, don't log on.

■ Do you want to send and receive messages automatically, on start-up and/or at regular intervals?

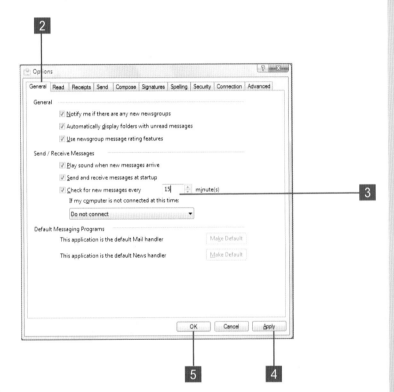

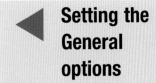

## Setting the General options

1 Open the Tools menu and select Options…

2 Make sure the General tab is at the front.

3 If you turn on the Check for new messages option, set the time interval.

4 Click Apply to save the settings but leave the box open.

or

5 Click OK to save your settings and close the box.

9

### Important !

When setting options remember that:
■ The defaults work perfectly well.
■ No option will do any damage.
■ Options can be set and changed at any time.

## Setting the Read options

The Read options control how incoming messages are handled. Key points to note here:

- Header lines are shown in bold until they have been marked as read. You can mark them yourself, using the Mark as Read command on the Edit menu, or you can have them marked automatically after a short delay.

- You can set the font in which messages are displayed. This will override whatever font – and font size – was used when the message was written.

**1** Open the Tools menu and select Options…

**2** Click the Read label to bring its tab to the front.

**3** If you turn on the Mark messages read… option, set a delay long enough to have a quick glance at a new message and decide whether you want to move on to the next new message and read this one later.

**4** To change the font or size, click Fonts….

**5** At the Fonts dialogue box, select the Proportional font and/or the Font size.

**6** Click Apply to save the settings.

or

**7** Click OK to save your settings and close the box.

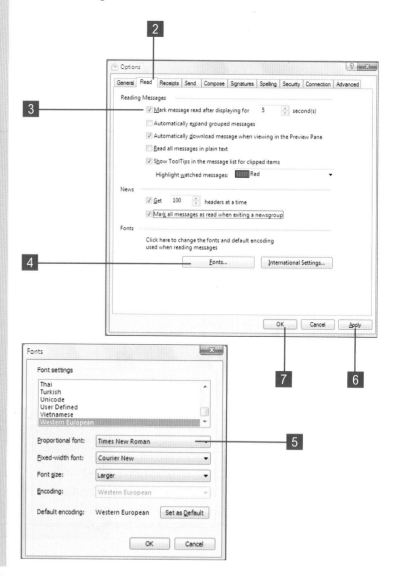

When you send an email, you can ask for a receipt to be sent when your recipient opens it. And, of course, incoming messages may have the same requests for receipts. This can all be done automatically. It's useful to let people know that you have received their message – though it does also rather require you to reply to it!

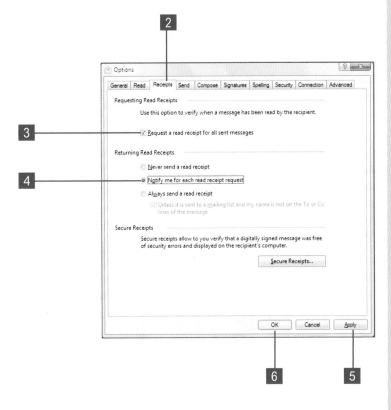

1. Open the Tools menu and select Options…

2. Click the Receipts label to bring its tab to the front.

3. If you want to know if your messages have got through, turn on the Request a read receipt option.

4. Decide how to handle requests from other people.

5. Click Apply to save the settings.

   or

6. Click OK to save your settings and close the box.

9

### For your information

Secure receipts are one aspect of protecting email privacy and security. They are only relevant if you have a digital signature – and you need valuable confidential data to protect to justify the subscription charges for one of those.

# Setting the Send options

1. Open the Tools menu and select Options...
2. Switch to the Send tab.
3. Set the options as required.
4. Click [ Apply ] to save the settings.

   or

5. Click [ OK ] to save your settings and close the box.

- Save copy of sent messages in the Sent Items folder – mainly for business users who need to keep a record of everything. If you need a copy of a message, save it before you send it.

- Send messages immediately – turn this on if you have broadband. If you dial-up to connect, turn this off, and use the Send/Receive button to send your messages in one batch.

- Automatically put people I reply to in my Address Book – is worth turning on, as it makes sure that you have their addresses. You can always delete unwanted ones later.

- Automatically complete email addresses when composing – worth turning on. When you are writing an email, you can enter someone's address by typing the name. With this on, you may only need to type two or three letters.

- Include messages in reply – best turned off, for home users. Business users may prefer to copy the original message into the reply, so that it can be answered point by point.

- Reply to messages using the format in which they were sent – should be turned on. This formats replies in plain text or HTML to match the incoming messages – so that you don't send HTML to people who can only handle Plain Text.

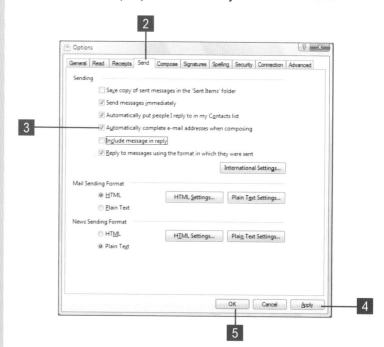

The Compose options set the defaults for the appearance of new messages. You can, of course, override these and choose different fonts or an alternative stationery style when you are writing any individual message.

If you want to turn on the Business Cards options, you must first go to Windows Contacts and create an entry for yourself. It is the details from this that are sent as a 'business card' file, attached to messages. Note that Outlook Express – the email software of many home users – cannot read other people's business cards. You may well not want to bother with this.

## Setting the Compose font

1 Open the Tools menu and select Options…

2 Switch to the Compose tab.

3 Click  Font Settings…  to the right of the Mail field.

4 Set the font and size as required and click  OK .

5 Repeat 3 and 4 for the News if you are active in any newsgroups.

6 Click  Select…  and set the default mail (and news) stationery, if required.

7 If you want to attach a business card to your messages, tick the Mail box, then pick your Contacts entry from the list.

8 Click  Apply  or  OK .

9

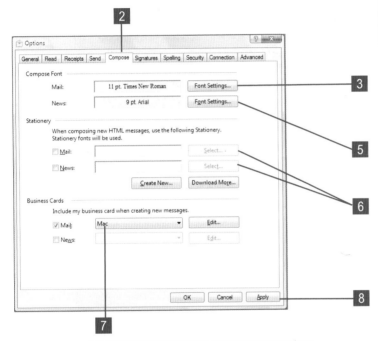

# Creating a signature

A signature is a short text file that can be added to the end of your messages. It might just be your name, phone number, street address and/or other contact details, or it could be more. In business the signature very often contains a disclaimer to the effect that the firm is not responsible for anything in the message. Some people like to add their motto or favourite quote, or a link to a selected website. It's your signature – use it how you like, but remember that your regular contacts will see it every time, and witty quotes can wear thin.

1  Open the Tools menu and select Options...

2  Switch to the Signatures tab.

3  Click New .

4  In the Edit Signature area, type the text that you want to include.

5  Click Apply to save the settings.

or

6  Click OK to save your settings and close the box.

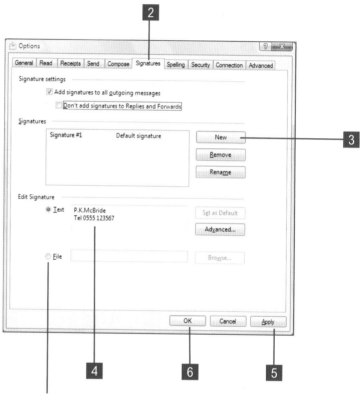

The File option allows you to use an existing text file as the signature – business users use this to add standard disclaimer text.

Not all of us are good spellers, and even the best make typing mistakes, but when you have a good spell checker at hand, there is really no excuse for sending badly-spelled (or typed) messages. The only questions should be whether or not you set the spell check to start automatically, and what sort of words do you want it to ignore.

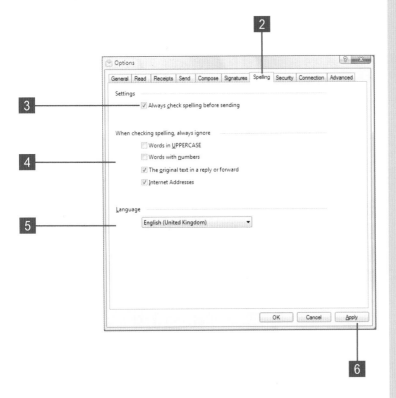

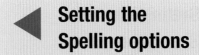
1. Open the Tools menu and select Options…

2. Switch to the Spelling tab.

3. If you want the checker to start automatically, turn on the Always check… option.

4. Tick the categories of words that you want the checker to ignore.

5. Check the Language setting is right – the default setting may well be English (United States).

6. Click Apply or OK .

9

# Setting the Security options

Security restricts. The more secure you make your system, the less chance there is that viruses and spyware will get in and cause damage, but equally, the less you will be able to do. The trick is to find a happy medium.

If you have a good ISP, they will run virus-checking software on all your email before it gets to your mailbox, and remove any viruses that they find. That is your first line of defence. The second line of defence is in the Security options. Go for the most secure settings at first, reducing the level only if you find it is too restricting.

**1** Open the Tools menu and select Options...

**2** Switch to the Security tab.

**3** In the Virus Protection area, select Restricted sites zone.

**4** Turn on Warn me when other applications try to send mail as me – there are viruses that do this.

**5** Turn on Do not allow attachments... – just in case you forget to take care!

**6** If you get a lot of spam mail, turn on Block images... – though this will also block pictures that your friends try to send you.

**7** If you want to know more about digital IDs, click Get Digital ID... and follow the link to an issuing website.

**8** Click Apply or OK.

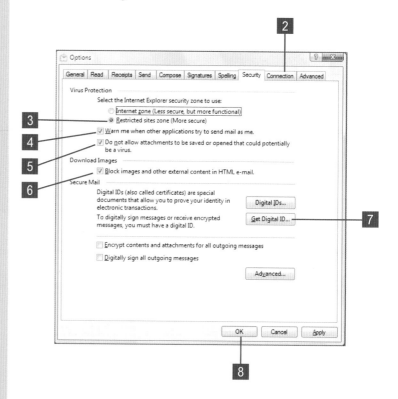

## Important

Digital IDs offer very secure email, but at a price. They are really only needed by business users with highly confidential information to protect.

There are only two real options here and both only apply to people who have dial-up connections rather than broadband:

- If you have more than one ISP – and there is often an overlap if you switch providers – you have to redial to pick up your mail from the other account. Do you want Windows Mail to check with you first?

- If you are charged by the minute for the online phone time, you will probably want to hang up after sending and collecting your mail.

## Setting the Connection options

1 Open the Tools menu and select Options…

2 Switch to the Connection tab.

3 If you have several connections, you may want to turn on Ask before switching…

4 Turn on Hang up after … if this suits the way you work online and saves you money.

5 If you want to change your connection settings, click Change… to open the Internet Properties dialogue box.

6 Click Apply or OK.

9

### See also

The Internet Properties dialogue box can also be reached through Internet Explorer. See page 96 for more on these settings.

# Setting the Maintenance options

The Maintenance options are there to help you keep things tidy. When messages are deleted, they are moved into the Deleted Items folder, and only erased when you delete them from there. You can get Windows Mail to empty Deleted Items when it closes down – I find this useful, but deleting 'by hand' does give you a second chance to think if you really want to keep a message.

Because of the way that email messages are stored, deleting does not itself free up disk space. It is only when you compact a folder that the disk space is reclaimed.

If you are active in any newsgroups, you can set when to delete read news messages.

1️⃣ Open the Tools menu and select Options…

2️⃣ Switch to the Advanced tab.

3️⃣ Click Maintenance… to open the Maintenance dialogue box.

4️⃣ Tick or clear the Empty messages from the Deleted Items … checkbox, as you prefer.

5️⃣ If you read newsgroup messages, decide when to have them deleted.

6️⃣ Click Clean Up Now… .

7️⃣ Select the folder to clean, then click Remove or Delete… to erase the messages (and their headers).

8️⃣ Wait for the routine to work, then click Close .

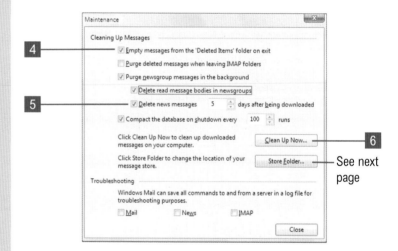

See next page

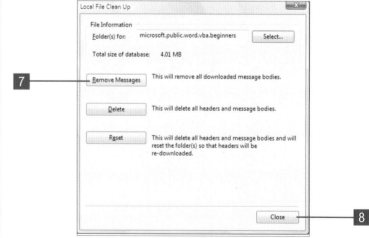

## Important

The other Advanced options are best left at their default settings.

The obvious question is, 'Why would I want to do this?' Most of the time, it's best to leave applications to take care of their own special files, but sometimes they mess up. If you find that messages can't be deleted, or that Window Mail does not respond properly to your attempts to manage folders and messages – and this situation can arise – then changing the store folder may be the answer. When you do this, Window Mail has to reorganise its storage, and in doing so it can remake the lost connections.

## Changing the store folder

1. If necessary, create the new folder in Windows Explorer.

2. Back in Windows Mail, open the Tools menu and select Options…

3. Go to the Maintenance tab.

4. Click Store Folder… to open the Store Location dialog box.

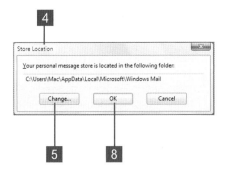

5. Click Change .

6. At the Browse for Folder dialogue box, the current folder will be highlighted. Scroll up and down as necessary to locate the new folder.

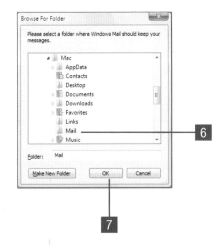

7. Click OK .

8. Back at the Store Location dialogue box, click OK .

9. The next time that you start Windows Mail, there will be a slight delay while it moves data into the new location.

# Avoiding information overload

Email is such a quick and easy way to communicate that it gets overused. Office workers today typically get five to ten times as many emails as they used to get memos, letters and phone calls – and they still get memos, letters and calls!

Emails you can do without include:

- From colleagues, 'I'm copying this to you to keep you in the loop on developments' – thanks but just tell me when I need to know!

- From hustlers, 'Make money fast!!' – you won't, but they might if they can find enough mugs.

- From friends, 'I thought you might like to see these photos from our holiday in Eastbourne' – and the photos are all 4 megapixels which means that (a) they are big files and take time to download – maybe overnight if you have a dial-up connection! – and (b) are so large that they won't fit on the screen.

The simplest way to deal with all of these is to select the messages by their subject/senders and delete them immediately.

- With over-enthusiastic photographers you could explain your problems of downloading messages and viewing big images.

- With over-inclusive colleagues you should try to get your organisation to adopt a policy of limiting emails.

- With spam senders, whatever you do, don't reply – it only encourages them. If you ask them to remove your name from their mailing list, it shows that the email address is active, and they are likely to send even more.

If junk mail is a significant problem – particularly if a lot is coming from the same source – you might like to set up a message rule to deal with it. We'll have a look at that in the next two pages.

**See also**

See 'Is email safe?' on page 29.

A message rule is an instruction to Windows Mail to look out for a certain type of message, and to deal with it automatically. Typically, the rule will pick up messages from a named sender and delete them immediately.

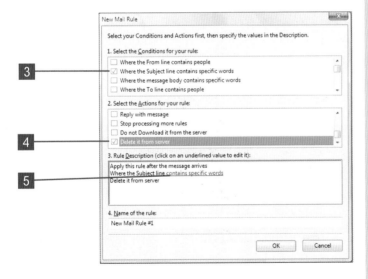

## Creating a message rule

1 On the Tools menu, point to Message Rules and select Mail… to open the Message Rules dialogue box.

2 Click New… .

3 Select the Condition for the rule – how are messages to be selected?

4 Select the Action – what is to be done with the messages?

5 If the condition needs to be defined – which people? which words? how big? – click on the underlined value.

9

## ! Important

If you do not yet have any rules, you will be taken directly to the New Mail Rule dialogue box when you first do this.

# Creating a message rule (cont.)

Most ISPs now run quite sophisticated spam filters that block a lot of junk mail, long before it reaches you. However, some gets through because there is no totally foolproof way to identify it. A good mail service will mark up likely junk mail by adding 'Spam', or something similar, to the Subject line.

In the same way, your message rules won't be able to block all spam, but if you get junk with common words in the Subject lines or from specific people, you can write rules to deal with those. For the rest, it is probably simpler to delete them by hand than to try to work out suitable rules.

**6** At the definition dialogue box, enter the values that you want the system to check for. You may need to enter several spellings of a word – if you want to block the stock market spammers, 'stock' isn't enough as they deliberately mis-spell to get round message rules!

**7** Click OK.

**8** Back at the Message Rules dialogue box, type a name for the rule.

**9** Click OK.

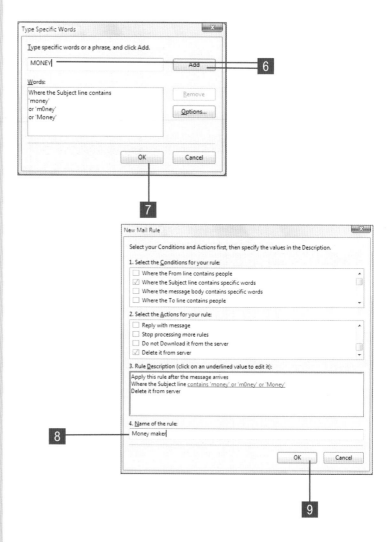

You can create a message rule from a message. This works best when the rule is based on the sender, and you want to move their new messages directly into a specific folder, rather than sitting in the Inbox.

If you want to block messages from them, use the Blocked Senders list – see the next page.

If you want to base the message on the Subject line, this approach is no better than the standard way.

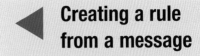

## Creating a rule from a message

**1** Select the message.

**2** On the Message menu, select Create Rule From Message…

**3** At the New Mail Rules dialogue box, select the Action.

**4** If the action needs to be defined click on the underlined value and supply the information.

**5** Click OK .

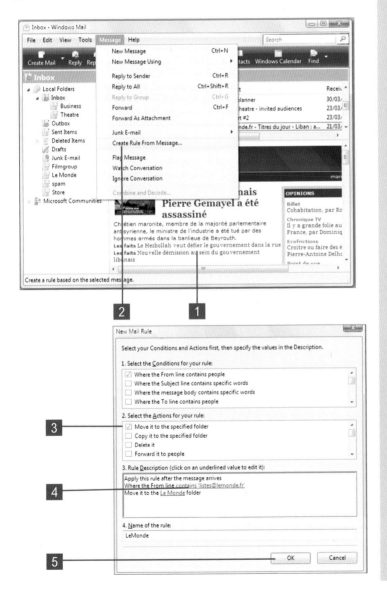

9

# Newsgroups

## Introduction

There are over 50,000 newsgroups running on the Internet, with new ones being started up every day. They are organised into a hierarchy with around twenty major (and many more minor) divisions, subdivided by topic, and subdivided again where necessary. Their names normally reflect this structure and describe the focus of their interest. For example, rec.arts.animation is found in the arts subdivision of the rec main division and is devoted to animation as an art form. (There are other animation groups elsewhere, with different focuses.) Sometimes, the dots are used for punctuation, and sometimes just for fun – there is, for instance one called alt.buddha.short.fat.guy!

Some groups are very active, with lots of messages every day and vigorous discussions. Others are much quieter, with only the occasional message trying to start a discussion or to find an answer to a problem. Take an hour or so to explore them for yourself – with so many groups, there is bound to be something there that will grab your attention.

## What you'll do

**Set up a news account**

**Explore the newsgroups**

**Go to a newsgroup**

**Read the news**

**Post to a newsgroup**

**Manage your subscriptions**

**Learn the netiquette**

**Use smileys and abbreviations**

# Setting up a news account

1. Run Windows Mail.
2. Open the Tools menu and select Accounts... to open the Internet Accounts dialogue box at the News tab.
3. Click Add... .
4. At the first stage of the wizard, select Newsgroup Account as the type to add.

Newsgroups can be accessed through the web, but they were designed to run over the email system, and that is the most efficient way to handle them. However, for you to be able to do this, your ISP must be actively involved – it has to collect newsgroup messages from their various origins and hold them in its computers ready for you to download. (As it does with email messages.) Most ISPs will usually handle a selection of newsgroups, filtering out those which are likely to be of very little interest to their users – e.g. Korean language groups in the UK – or which are mainly used to circulate porn (and there are a lot of those!).

To find out what newsgroups your ISP can offer, you first need to set up a newsgroup account, and then download the list of groups.

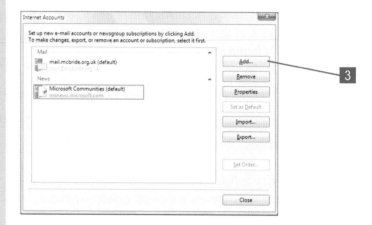

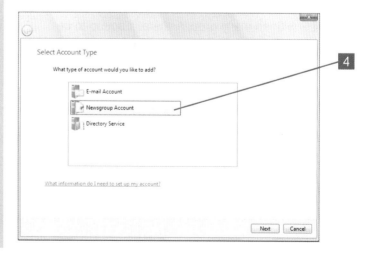

To set up a news account you will need to know the name of the news server at your ISP. Your ISP may have supplied you with the name in your start-up pack, or it may be easy to find out at the site. If not, you can probably work it out easily enough. Normally, the name will be 'news' followed by the ISP's domain name. For example, Virgin's domain name is 'virgin.net' – and we can work this out because their website address is 'www.virgin.net', so their news server is probably called 'news.virgin.net'. And it is.

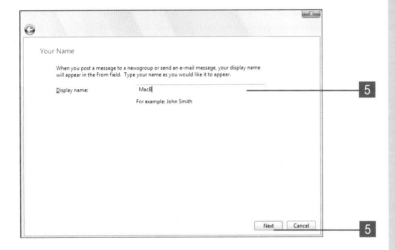

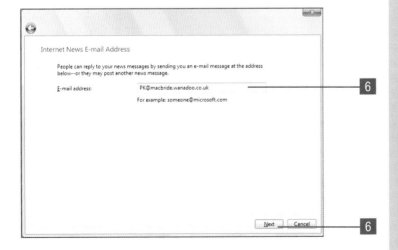

5 Type the name that you would like to appear on any messages you post to newsgroups. Click Next >

6 At the next step enter your email address. Click Next >.

10

# Setting up a news account (cont.)

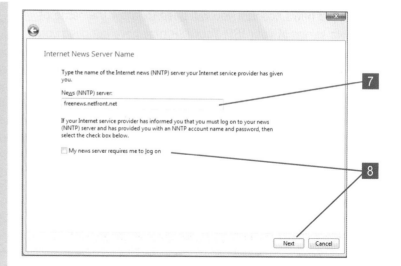

**7** Type in the name for the news server.

**8** Leave My news server requires me to log on clear – it almost certainly doesn't. And if it does, we can sort this out later. Click Next >.

**9** Click Finish.

**10** Click Close.

**11** You will be asked if you want to download newsgroups for the account – you do. If you are on a standard phone line, and your ISP offers a decent set of groups, this could take a while!

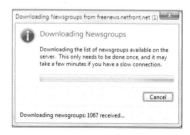

The Newsgroup Subscription dialogue box has three tabs:

- All lists all the newsgroups held on the server – browse through it sometime, just to see the range and variety.

- The Subscribed tab lists those to which you are currently subscribed – these will also be in the Folders list.

- New shows any newsgroups which have been added since you last contacted the server.

On any panel, you can subscribe to a group by selecting it and clicking Subscribe. Subscribing to a newsgroup brings it into your news folder for easy access and makes it available for synchronising (see page 243). If, after sampling a group, you decide that it is not for you, you can unsubscribe at any point.

Before you can subscribe to a group, you have to find it. That is easier than it might appear when you first see that list! Into the box Display newsgroups which contain, type a word that might appear in the newsgroup's name, and the list will reset to display only those containing the word.

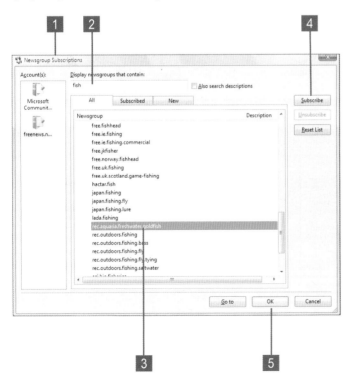

## Subscribe to a newsgroup

**1** Open the Tools menu and select Newsgroups… to open the Newsgroup Subscriptions dialogue box.

**2** Enter one or more words to describe what interests you in the Display newsgroups which contain slot.

**3** Scroll through the list and select a newsgroup.

**4** Click Subscribe. The groups will be added to a list below your news server account in the Folder list.

**5** Repeat steps 2–4 to add any other groups then click OK.

Simply subscribing does not bring in any messages from the groups. That is a separate job, which we will come back to shortly (see page 241).

10

# Going to a newsgroup

You can also sample a group using the Go to button at the bottom of the dialogue box. Click this to dip into a group, to see what's there, without adding it to your list of subscribed groups, or to catch up with the news in your favourite groups while working on someone else's computer. When you Go to a newsgroup, you can read its articles during that session, but the link will be discarded when you close down Windows Mail.

1 Open the Newsgroups Subscription dialogue box and get a list of groups which might interest you.

2 Select a newsgroup.

3 Click ⌈ Go to ⌋.

4 The group will be added to your news server folder, and the headers of any current messages will be loaded into the Header pane of Windows Mail. You are ready to start reading the news. On to the next page!

## Timesaver tip

If an article has a file attached to it, you can save or open it in the same way as a file attached to a mail message.

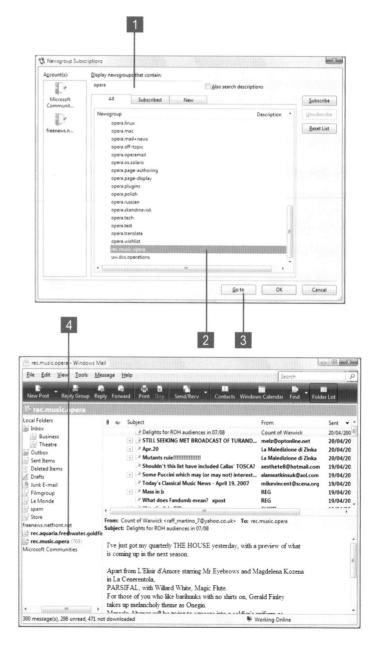

A newsgroup may generate anything from 2 to 200 articles or messages every day. Even if you are fascinated by the topic of the newsgroup, you are unlikely to want to read every article, and that is where the subject line helps. Unlike email, where the headers and body text of new messages are downloaded together, with newsgroups, only the headers are normally downloaded at first. The body text doesn't follow until you select a message from the header lines – one reason why a clear subject is essential in newsgroup articles.

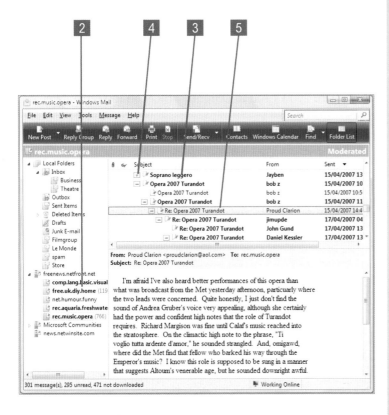

## Reading the news

1 If you used ⬚Go to⬚ to sample the newsgroup, the Header pane will already be displaying the current headers.

2 If you have subscribed to a group, click on it in the Folder list to download the headers.

3 Scan through the subjects in the header lines to find out what the articles are about.

4 Click ⊞ to expand threads so that you can see the follow-up articles.

5 Click on an article to read it in the Preview pane.

**Jargon buster**

**Thread** – a series of replies to an article, and the replies to the replies – and so on ad infinitum.

10

# Posting to a newsgroup

1 Select the article.

2 Click the appropriate reply button. The Compose window will open, with the header lines filled in for you.

3 Edit the original text down, to focus on the parts you want to reply to.

4 Type your reply.

5 Click .

## See also

Do not rush into posting to a newsgroup. And take the time to learn the netiquette before you post – see page 244.

You can respond to an article in two ways – send an email to the author only, or post a follow-up article to the group. In general, if the original article was a request for information and not likely to be of general interest, reply to the author. If you want to follow up with your own contribution to the discussion, you should quote the relevant lines from the original article or give a summary of the key points that you want to pick up. There are three reply and forward buttons:

■ Reply Group posts an article to the group, adding it to the thread.

■ Reply posts an email message to the author.

■ Forward allows you to send the article on to someone else.

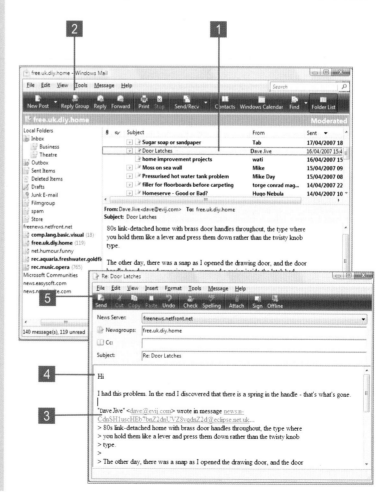

If you only subscribe to one or two newsgroups, they don't need much management – just click on the group to get the latest headers, then click to read a few selected articles.

If you make more use of newsgroups than this – and some people do find them a good way to interact with fellow enthusiasts – then you might want to make more use of the synchronisation facilities. You can set up your subscribed newsgroups so that with one click the system will download all their messages, or just the new ones, or the headers.

With busy newsgroups, where only a few of the messages are likely to be of interest, you can get the headers, skim through these, marking those you want to read, then download the marked messages. If you are paying for phone time, this is the most efficient way to read the news.

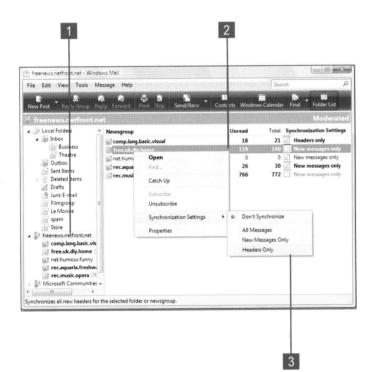

## Managing your subscriptions

1 Click on the news server name in the Folder list.

2 In the Synchronisation pane, select a newsgroup.

3 Right-click on a newsgroup, point to Synchronisation Settings, and make your choice. Select what you want to be downloaded when you use the Synchronisation routine. New messages only would be the normal choice; All messages is useful the first time that you access a group; Headers only is good where the groups tends to have large messages (perhaps containing files) and you normally only open a few.

Repeat steps 2 and 3 for all your newsgroups.

4 Open the Tools menu and select Synchronise Account (or All) to get the latest headers/messages.

5 Next time you want to pick up the latest from your groups, you use Tools, Synchronise All instead of working from the Synchronisation pane, if you like.

10

# Learning the netiquette

Like much of the rest of the Internet, the newsgroup system relies on cooperation, voluntary labour, sponsorship and a set of agreed rules – its netiquette. Take the trouble to learn the rules and use them.

Using netiquette is not just about being a good news user – it is also a matter of self-preservation. You must remember that, in a popular group, any article you write is going to be downloaded by several thousand people, and many of these will be paying phone and online charges for receiving your article. If you waste their time and money, they will not be happy and may well respond with **flames**. Follow the rules and make life easier for others and for yourself.

- When you first join a newsgroup, **lurk**.

- Do KISS – Keep It Short and Simple. Keep it short to save phone time; keep it simple because the Internet is international and not all users are native English-speakers.

- Do top and tail thoughtfully. Write a clear and descriptive subject line, and keep your signature short.

- Do be relevant. Every newsgroup has its own focus; and straying off-topic will get you **flamed**.

- Do read any follow-ups to an article before writing yours. Someone else may already have made the same points.

- Do summarise, or crop the original article when replying.

- Don't overreact. Ignore bad spelling and poor grammar – this is a multilingual community; if you spot mistakes, drop the writer an email, don't humiliate him or her in public; if you are angered by an offensive article, wait until you are calm, and write a reasoned rebuttal.

- Don't try irony or subtle jokes – they don't travel well – but smileys can lighten a comment (see page 245).

- Don't advertise, except in newsgroups that are for this purpose – 'for sales', business announcements, etc.

- Don't post reviews of books or films that reveal the plot, or jokes that might offend tender sensibilities, without first scrambling the article with **rot13**.

## Jargon buster

**Lurking** – reading, without posting – so that you can get a feel of what the group is about.

**Flames** – bad tempered emails, typically sent by the more aggressive members of a group when someone has made a particularly stupid or unacceptable remark.

**rot13** – a simple coding system that substitutes each letter with the one 13 along (wrapping round from Z back to A). It hides the meaning of a message from casual glances. There is an Unscramble option on the Message menu if you need it.

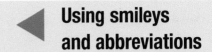

## Smileys

Being good news users (and perhaps indifferent typists?), we try to keep our articles short – abbreviations help here. But as we keep them short, and as we may not know our potential readers very well, if at all, there is a chance of our attempts at humour being misunderstood. Smileys were developed to help overcome this.

Smileys are little pictures, made up of typed characters, which are intended to replace the facial expressions that we use to convey the emotions or hidden meanings behind what we say. The basic smiley of **:-)** is the one you will see most often, though there are many other weird and wonderful smileys around. There is a small selection on the left – look out for more when you are reading your mail and news articles.

## Abbreviations

These are mainly used in real-time conferences and chat lines, though some crop up quite regularly in newsgroup articles. If you want to track down more abbreviations or the acronyms used elsewhere in the computing world, an excellent list called Babel is maintained by Irving and Richard Kind at Columbia University in the States. You can read it at this URL:

http://www.geocities.com/ikind_babel/babel/babel.html

## Emphasis

Articles for newsgroups should be written in plain text – no formatting – for the benefit of readers working on older or simpler systems. This means that you cannot underline or embolden words. If you want to make a word stand out, enclose it in *asterisks* or _underscores_, or use CAPITALS. But don't write whole articles in capitals. This is known as 'SHOUTING' and is much frowned upon!

---

### Some smileys

| | |
|---|---|
| :-) | The basic smiley, |
| '-) | Wink – 'Only joking!' |
| :-( | Frowning or sad |
| :-o | Wow! |
| :-| | Grim |
| :-C | 'I do not believe it!' |
| %-) | User has been staring at the screen for hours |

### Abbreviations

| | |
|---|---|
| BTW | By The Way |
| BWQ | Buzz Word Quotient |
| DL | DownLoad |
| FYI | For Your Information |
| GIGO | Garbage In Garbage Out |
| IMO | In My Opinion |
| IMHO | In My Humble Opinion (typically used ironically) |
| POV | Point Of View |
| RTFM | Read The F***ing Manual |
| TIA | Thanks In Advance |
| TTFN | Ta Ta For Now |
| UL | UpLoad |
| WRT | With Reference To |

10

# Creating a website

## 11

## Introduction

Most ISPs offer to host their members' websites, i.e. provide the space in which to store the files, and link the pages into the World Wide Web. They will usually also offer tools and advice to help you create the pages for your site, and to upload those pages to their computers.

Building a website is not that difficult, as long as you don't need anything fancier than formatted text and images on the pages, with a straightforward set of links between them. The pages can be created from 'scratch' – writing the HTML code directly, which is far easier than you might at first expect. They can also be produced through a number of different applications, which we will not be looking at here as they are fairly specialised, and by Word, which we will have a brief look at.

## What you'll do

**Plan a website**

**Understand HTML tags**

**Create your index page**

**View your index page**

**Format text**

**Set colours**

**Set the text size**

**Draw a line**

**Make a list**

**Create hyperlinks**

**Display an image**

**Link a thumbnail to an image**

**Link pages into a website**

**Add keywords in a META tag**

**Upload your files**

**Create a web page in Word**

**Format text in Word**

**Create a link in Word**

**Follow links in Word**

# Planning a website

The hardest parts of creating a website are deciding what to publish and how to present it. Compared with these, the mechanics of putting pages together is quite simple!

- Who are the pages for? Friends and family, fellow fans or others with shared interests, potential customers? The more you are trying to attract new people to your site, the more care you must take over its design.

- If a page is mainly text, can it be conveniently broken up into screen-sized chunks? People do not like scrolling through long pages to get to the bit that interests them. On the other hand, if it is continuous text – a story or article – then it is better to present it on one long page. This makes it easier for your visitors to save it for reading offline later.

- Images add to the attractiveness of pages, but they add to download time. Think about why and how you use them.

- Your web pages will be viewed in different sizes of windows. Screens range from $1920 \times 1200$ to $640 \times 480$ pixels, and people may not run their browsers at full screen. A page which looks good on your big screen, may not work in a small window.

- Aim for a clean, unfussy design, with a good contrast between the text and background colours, and readable-sized text, with headings that are large enough to be noticeable without dominating the screen.

- How will you structure your material? You shouldn't try to put too much on a single page, so for anything other than the simplest page, you must think about how it can be organised.

## Structuring a website

The top page is normally called 'index.htm', though this is not needed in the address. When you type 'www.mysite.com' into the browser, it actually looks for 'www.mysite.com/index.htm'.

A very simple website might have all its text and images on that top page. At the next level, the site would use index.htm to carry its welcome information and links to the other pages – and that is the sort of site that we will be building in this chapter. More complex sites could have several levels of menus, with links criss-crossing between the pages.

### Important

!

On some servers, the top page must be called 'index.html'. Check with your ISP before you upload your files.

In HTML, all styling is done with tags – codes which tell the browser how to display text or images. These are mainly in pairs, one at each end of whatever is being styled. They follow simple rules:

- A tag is always enclosed in <angle brackets>.

- The opening and closing tags of each pair are identical except for a / before the identifier in the end tag.

- Tags can be written in either capitals or lower case.

- Tags can be on the same line as the enclosed text, or on separate lines – it makes no difference to the appearance in the browser.

For example, to get a third level heading – 14 point bold type – the tags are <H3> and </H3>. So you would write:

    <h3>This is a sub-head</h3>

or, remembering the last two rules, you could write it like this:

    <H3>
    This is a sub-head
    </H3>

Both produce this same effect:

## This is a sub-head

Use whichever form is easiest to read in your text file.

### Commonly used tags

    <HTML>...</HTML>

Mark the start and end of the HTML file.

    <HEAD> ... </HEAD>

Mark the header area, that will hold the title and information about the page, which search engines can use to identify the nature and contents of the page.

The remainder of the text is the body and is enclosed by:

    <BODY> ...</BODY>

This holds the code for the visible page.

    <TITLE> ... </TITLE>

Whatever is marked as the title is displayed in the window's title bar.

## Important

An HTML file is plain text, and can be created in any editor or word processor that can output plain ASCII text – WordPad or Notepad (they should both be on the Accessories menu in Windows) are ideal. You can also get Word to produce web pages directly – letting it write the tags for you. We'll look at that later on in this chapter.

## Creating your index page

The first page anyone meets on your site will be the index page, so let's start by creating that. We'll actually do this in stages. At first we will set up a very simple page, then come back later to add links to it so that you can move from the index page to the others once you have created them.

This is my page. Yours should have the same structure and tags, but with your own words for the title and heading:

1 Set up a new folder for your home page files. You will be saving all the pages and images here.

2 Start NotePad, WordPad, Word – whichever you prefer.

3 Type in the HTML text shown here, customised to suit you.

4 Open the File menu and select Save.

5 Locate your home page folder.

6 Save the document as a text file with the name 'index.htm'.

7 Click Save.

```
<HTML>
<HEAD>
<TITLE>Mac's web site</title>
</HEAD>

<BODY>
<H1>Welcome to my site</H1>
</BODY>
</HTML>
```

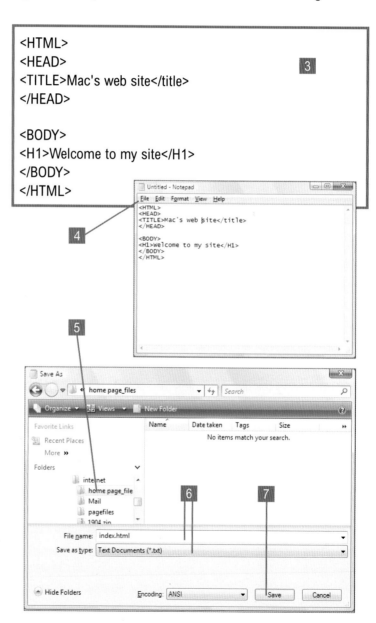

## Important

Web page files can have .htm or .html extensions. Some ISPs insist that your top level page is called index.html – with an 'L'. Check the rules at your ISP.

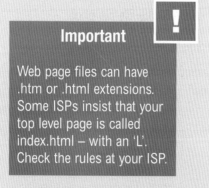

In this early stage of construction, your 'website' will remain located on your computer, and you will be the only one who will be able to see it. Later, you will upload the completed pages and image files to your web space at your ISP's site – and then it will be on the web.

Meanwhile, you can still view your pages in Internet Explorer using its File, Open command.

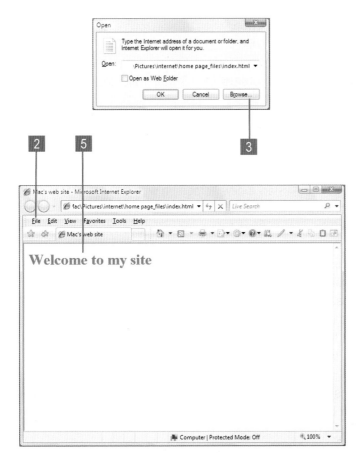

**1** Switch to, or start Internet Explorer. You do not need to be online, but it won't matter if you are.

**2** Open the File menu and select Open.

**3** At the Open dialogue box, click Browse... .

**4** Look in the website folder and open your index.htm file.

**5** Check the display and return to the editor to enhance and improve the text file!

### Timesaver tip

It is quick and easy to see the effects of changes in your HTML file. Keep Internet Explorer and the editor windows open, and after each change to the text, save the HTML file again, then click ↔ to reload the new version into Internet Explorer.

## Formatting text

1. Start a new file in your editor.
2. Type in the sample text shown on the page opposite, replacing my words with yours if you like, but keeping the tags and the structure.
3. Save the file as 'text.htm'.

**Timesaver tip**

If your formatting tags don't seem to be doing the job properly, check that each opening <TAG> has a matching closing </TAG> – and that it is in the right place.

**Important**

Remember that Internet Explorer is not the only browser. Though all browsers can read and display HTML pages, there are some minor differences in how they interpret some HTML tags. Professional web builders always check the appearance of their sites on different browsers.

The simplest tags are the ones that format text. These will produce six levels of headings, a small, italicised style (mainly used for email addresses), and bold and italic for emphasis.

| | | |
|---|---|---|
| <H1> | </H1> | # Heading 1 |
| <H2> | </H2> | ## Heading 2 |
| <H3> | </H3> | ### Heading 3 |
| <H4> | </H4> | Heading 4 |
| <H5> | </H5> | Heading 5 |
| <H6> | </H6> | Heading 6 |
| <B> | </B> | **Bold** |
| <I> | </I> | *Italic* |
| <Address> | </Address> | *Small italic style* |

The Heading and Address tags break the text up into separate lines, but untagged text appears as a continuous stream. Create separate paragraphs with these tags:

**<P></P>**  Start a new paragraph with a space before and after

**<BR>**  Start a new line without a space before it

When a browser reads an HTML file, it ignores all spaces (apart from a single one between words), and **[Enter]** key presses. It doesn't matter how you lay out your HTML text – you can indent it, and add line breaks to make it easier to read, but it won't affect what your visitors see – only the tags affect the layout of the page in the browser.

Tags can sometimes be combined. For example, you can make text bold like this:

    <B>This is bold</B>

or make it italic like this:

    <I>This is italic</I>

or apply both bold and italics like this:

    <I><B>This is bold and italics</B></I>

When you combine tags, you must nest them – write one pair inside the other.

```
<HTML>
<HEAD>
<TITLE>Formatting text</TITLE>
</HEAD>

<BODY>
<H1>Formatting text</H1>
<H2>Using header tags…</H2>
<H6>…though headers can be rather small</H6>
<BR>
And some plain text, here after a break.
<P>and here using the paragraph tag to leave a space
above the paragraph</P>
<P>We can make things stand out in <B>bold</B> or
<I>italics</I> or <B><I>both</I></B></P>
<P>
<ADDRESS>This page was made by me </ADDRESS>
</BODY>
</HTML>
```

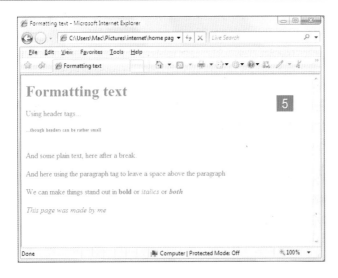

4 Switch to the Internet Explorer window and use the File, Open command to load in your new page.

5 Check for errors. Are there any typos in the text? Is it formatted as it should be?

6 If necessary, edit and resave the HTML file, then refresh the browser display.

### Important

Internet Explorer has a grey background by default. Use the Tools, Internet Options to set it to white so that you can read your text more easily.

# Setting colours

Text-only pages are fast to load, but can be a bit boring. Colour adds impact to your screens, without adding to the loading time.

Colours can be defined in two ways. The simplest is to use standard colour names. All browsers, of any type and age, can recognise and respond to these names in HTML pages:

| Black | Grey | White | Navy Blue |
| Blue | Green | Lime | Maroon |
| Red | Turquoise | Purple | Olive |
| Aqua | Fuchsia | Yellow | |

Newer browsers can also interpret a wider range of colour names, but these should be enough for most purposes.

1. Start a new file in your editor.
2. Type in the sample text shown on the page opposite, varying colours as you like.
3. Save the file as 'colours.htm'.
4. Open the file in Internet Explorer to see how it looks.

Colours can also be defined by the values of their Red, Green and Blue components – given in that order and in hexadecimal digits. These values can be anything from 00 to FF, but are best set at 00 (off), 80 (half/dark) or FF (full power/bright), e.g.:

    FFFF00

gives Red and Green at full, with no Blue, resulting in Yellow. Combinations of 00, 80 and FF values should come out true on all screens. Intermediate values, giving more subtle shades of colours, may not always be displayed properly.

## BODY colours

The BODY tag can have extra information written into it to set the colours of the background and text of the page. The option keywords are BGCOLOR and TEXT and are set like this:

    <BODY BGCOLOR = "black" TEXT = "white">

## FONT colours

At any point on the page, you can change the colour of the text with the tag:

    <FONT COLOR = "colour name" >

The colour is used for all following text until it is reset with another <FONT COLOR = ... > tag. You can use it to pick out words within normal text – though you can get strange results if you use the tags inside Headings.

The closing </FONT> tag can be omitted. If you use it, the text colour will revert to what it was before the opening <FONT COLOR = ... > tag.

## Did you know?

You must have a good contrast in shade – as well as in hue – between your text colours and the background colour. If they are too close together the page will be hard to read.

```
<HTML>
<HEAD>                                              2
<TITLE>Colours</TITLE>
</HEAD>

<BODY BGCOLOR = "white" TEXT = "navy blue">
<H1>Colours</H1>
<H2>
<FONT COLOR = red> Changing to red <BR>
<FONT COLOR = orange> Changing to orange <BR>
<FONT COLOR = yellow> Changing to yellow <BR>
<FONT COLOR = green> Changing to green <BR>
<FONT COLOR = blue> Changing to blue <BR>
<FONT COLOR = maroon> Changing to maroon <BR>
<FONT COLOR = fuchsia> Changing to fuchsia<BR>
</FONT> and back to maroon<BR>
</FONT> and back to blue
</H2>
</BODY>
</HTML>
```

### Instant Hex

Read this if you want to set colours with hexadecimal values.

All modern numbering systems are founded on 'place value' – how much a digit stands for depends upon its place in the figure. 42 means $4 \times 10 + 2$. In hexadecimal, the place multiplier is 16, rather than 10. So 42 in hex is worth $4 \times 16 + 2 = 66$ in normal base-10 system.

To make hex work, more digits are needed – 0 1 2 3 4 5 6 7 8 9 A B C D E F – with A to F standing for the values 10 to 15 in the base-10 system.

Hex is used in computing because it is compact – you can represent any number for 0 to 255 in two digits ($FF = 15 \times 16 + 15 = 255$) – and because there is a simple conversion between hex and binary, the native numbering system of computer chips.

### Important

Note the US spelling COLOR – COLOUR will not work!

## Setting the text size

The <FONT> tag can take a number of other options as well as COLOR, and one which you really should know about is SIZE. This option takes a value between 1 and 7 and sets the size of the text as follows: 1 = 8 point, 2 = 10 point, 3 = 12 point, 4 = 14 point, 5 = 18 point, 6 = 24 point, 7 = 36 point.

You can use this at the start to set the size of the text for the whole page, or at any point within it. You can even vary the size within paragraphs, to make words really stand out, or for special effects.

1 Start a new file in your editor.

2 Type in the code shown here, using your own words for font size samples.

3 Save the file as 'fontsize.htm'.

4 Open the file in Internet Explorer to see how it looks.

```
<HTML>
<HEAD>
<TITLE>Font size</TITLE>
</HEAD>
<BODY>
<H1>Font size</H1>
<FONT SIZE = 1>This is font size 1</FONT><BR>
<FONT SIZE = 2>This is font size 2</FONT><BR>
<FONT SIZE = 3>This is font size 3</FONT><BR>
<FONT SIZE = 4>This is font size 4</FONT><BR>
<FONT SIZE = 5>This is font size 5</FONT><BR>
<FONT SIZE = 6>This is font size 6</FONT><BR>
<FONT SIZE = 7>This is font size 7</FONT><BR>
</BODY>
</HTML>
```

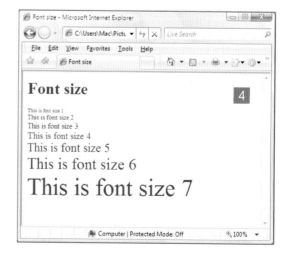

Lines, or Horizontal Rules, are created with the tag <HR>. This is a single tag – there is no </HR> to end it. A simple <HR> produces a thin 3D-effect line. For variety, use the options:

SIZE to set the thickness. This is measured in pixels. e.g.

    <HR SIZE = 6>

WIDTH can also be set in pixels or as a percentage of the width of the browser window, e.g.

    <HR WIDTH = 100>
    <HR SIZE = 6 WIDTH = 50%>

NOSHADE makes the line solid, e.g.

    <HR SIZE = 6 WIDTH = 250  NOSHADE>

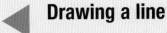

1 Start a new file in your editor.

2 Type in this sample text, varying the SIZE, WIDTH and NOSHADE options as you like.

3 Save the file as 'lines.htm'.

4 Open the file in Internet Explorer to see how it looks.

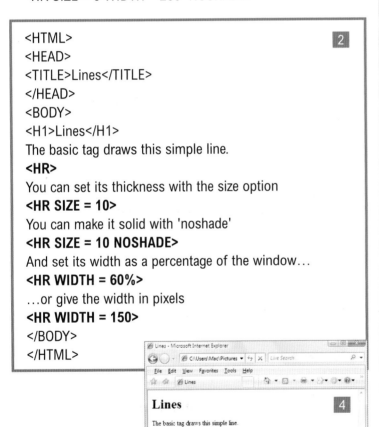

```
<HTML>                                    2
<HEAD>
<TITLE>Lines</TITLE>
</HEAD>
<BODY>
<H1>Lines</H1>
The basic tag draws this simple line.
<HR>
You can set its thickness with the size option
<HR SIZE = 10>
You can make it solid with 'noshade'
<HR SIZE = 10 NOSHADE>
And set its width as a percentage of the window…
<HR WIDTH = 60%>
…or give the width in pixels
<HR WIDTH = 150>
</BODY>
</HTML>
```

# Making a list

There are two types of lists. Both are constructed in the same way.

- ■ <OL> </OL> (ordered/numbered) or <UL> </UL> (unordered/bulleted) tags enclose the whole list.
- ■ Each item in the list is enclosed by <LI> </LI> tags, e.g.

```
<UL>
    <LI> List item </LI>
    <LI> List item </LI>
</UL>
```

Bullets are normally round. You can set the style to SQUARE with the TYPE option, e.g.

```
<UL TYPE = SQUARE>
```

**1** Start a new file in your editor.

**2** Type in this sample code, varying the text.

**3** Save the file as 'lists.htm'.

**4** Open the file in Internet Explorer to see how it looks.

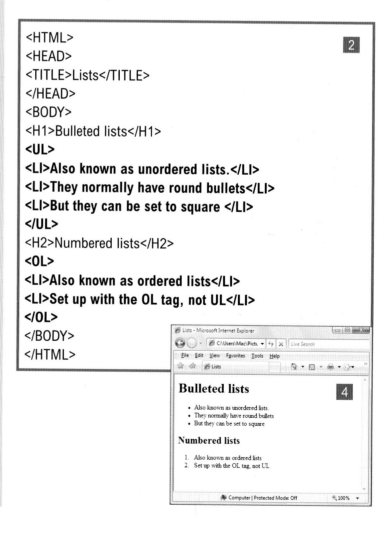

```
<HTML>                                                    2
<HEAD>
<TITLE>Lists</TITLE>
</HEAD>
<BODY>
<H1>Bulleted lists</H1>
<UL>
<LI>Also known as unordered lists.</LI>
<LI>They normally have round bullets</LI>
<LI>But they can be set to square </LI>
</UL>
<H2>Numbered lists</H2>
<OL>
<LI>Also known as ordered lists</LI>
<LI>Set up with the OL tag, not UL</LI>
</OL>
</BODY>
</HTML>
```

## Different types of lists

Unordered lists can have solid (the default) or open circles, or square bullets. To change the type of bullet, use the TYPE option like this:

| | |
|---|---|
| <UL TYPE = square> | square bullets |
| <UL TYPE = circle> | open circles |
| <UL TYPE = disc> | solid round bullets |

Ordered lists can have letters or Roman numerals, and both can be in capitals or lower case. Set the options like this:

| | |
|---|---|
| <OL TYPE = A> | Capital letters, e.g. A, B, C |
| <OL TYPE = a> | Lower case letters, e.g. a, b, c |
| <OL TYPE = I> | Roman numerals, in capital, e.g. I, II, III |
| <OL TYPE = i> | Roman numerals, in lower case, e.g. i, ii, iii |

1 Start a new file.

2 Type in the sample code, but with your own example text.

3 Save the file as 'listtypes.htm'.

4 Open it in Internet Explorer to see how it looks.

```
<HTML>                                          2
<HEAD>
<TITLE>List types</title>
</HEAD>

<BODY BGColor = white text = black>
<H1>Bulleted lists</H1>
<UL TYPE = circle>
<LI>This has square bullets.</LI>
<LI>And it has a numbered list nested inside it</LI>
<H2>Numbered lists</H2>
<OL TYPE = I>
<LI>This ordered list has letters</LI>
<LI>You can also have Roman numerals</LI>
</OL>
<LI>And back to the bulleted list</LI>
</UL>
</BODY>
</HTML>
```

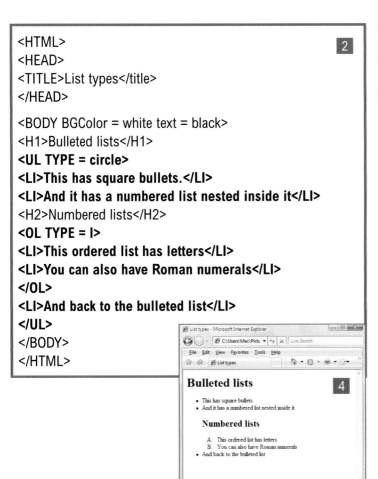

# Creating hyperlinks

Hyperlinks are the most important aspect of hypertext – without them, the web simply wouldn't exist. There are two parts to a hyperlink – it must define the page or file that is being linked, and mark the text or image that will be clicked to activate the jump. The basic shape is:

```
<A HREF=where_to_link> clickable_object </A>
```

The clickable_object can be a word or phrase – by itself or embedded in other text – or an image. Hyperlinked text is usually coloured and underlined, and images are normally outlined. Here we are using text – we'll add hyperlinks to images on page 263.

where_to_link can be the name of another page on your site:

```
<A HREF="products.htm"> Product list </A>
```

or the URL of a page somewhere else on the web:

```
<A HREF="http://www.yahoo.co.uk"> Go to Yahoo! </A>
```

1 Start a new file in your editor.

2 Type in this sample code, using your own choice of web addresses.

3 Save the file as 'links.htm'.

4 Open the file in Internet Explorer to see how it looks.

5 Go online, if necessary, and click on the links to check that they work. (And come straight back once you reach a site – the aim is to test the links, not to go surfing!)

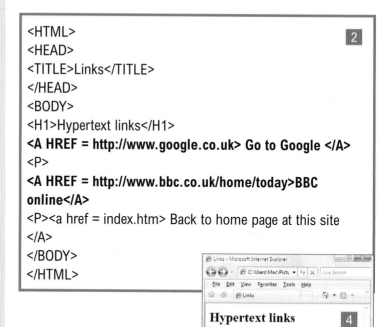

```
<HTML>                                              2
<HEAD>
<TITLE>Links</TITLE>
</HEAD>
<BODY>
<H1>Hypertext links</H1>
<A HREF = http://www.google.co.uk> Go to Google </A>
<P>
<A HREF = http://www.bbc.co.uk/home/today>BBC online</A>
<P><a href = index.htm> Back to home page at this site </A>
</BODY>
</HTML>
```

To display an image on a web page it must be in the right format. Browsers can only handle JPG and GIF images.

You can specify the size of an image in the browser, whatever its real size, e.g. you could set a 1,200 by 800 image to be displayed at 300 by 200 pixels. You can also set it to be a certain percentage of the window size, so that it always occupies the same relative amount of space, whatever the size of the page. The actual size of the image should not be more than the maximum size at which it is displayed. Images add to the download time, especially for those on dial-up connections, and over-large images slow things down needlessly.

To get your images into the right size and the right format, you will need some form of image processing software. If you have a digital camera, it probably came with some suitable software. If not, there are plenty of good shareware graphics programs out there. All you need is something which can handle different file formats, including JPG and GIF, and which can resize images.

The basic image tag is:

    <IMG SRC = "filename">

You can also use these options:

    ALIGN = "left/center/right"
    ALT = "description"
    WIDTH = value
    HEIGHT = value

**ALIGN** sets the position of the image across the page. Note the US spelling 'center'. The UK spelling 'centre' will not work!

**ALT** is the text to display if the image is not loaded into a browser, and also the tip that will appear if you pause the pointer over the image. In the example overleaf, if image loading was turned off, you would see this: 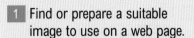 .

**WIDTH** and **HEIGHT** set the size of the image in the page. You can set the size as a percentage of either the width or height, or set it in pixels, giving both the width and the height.

    <IMG SRC="tiddles.jpg" ALT = "this is my cat" WIDTH = 80%>

This will display a picture of Tiddles, shrinking – or expanding – the image size so that it fills 80% of the width of the window.

1  Find or prepare a suitable image to use on a web page.

2  Start a new file in your editor.

3  Create a page along the lines shown overleaf, using your file and with suitable heading and ALT text.

4  Save the file as 'images.htm'.

5  Open the file in Internet Explorer. How does it look? What happens if you change the size of the Internet Explorer window?

**Did you know?**

If you set the image width to 100%, it will be resized to fit the browser window, whatever size it may be.

## Displaying an image (cont.)

**6** Edit the code to set the image at 80% of the screen width. You will need to add this in the <IMG SRC ...> tag

WIDTH = 80%

**7** Save the file and reload it into the browser to see the effect.

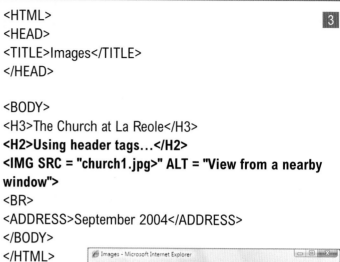

```
<HTML>
<HEAD>
<TITLE>Images</TITLE>
</HEAD>

<BODY>
<H3>The Church at La Reole</H3>
<H2>Using header tags...</H2>
<IMG SRC = "church1.jpg>" ALT = "View from a nearby
window">
<BR>
<ADDRESS>September 2004</ADDRESS>
</BODY>
</HTML>
```

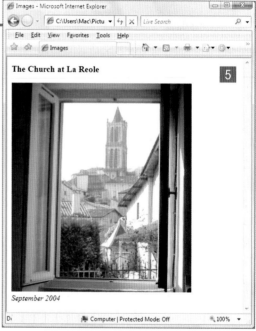

If you have a set of large photos that you want to share with your friends and family, you could do this by emailing copies of all of them to all of your circle. This may not always be welcome. Even on broadband, it could take a while for a lot of emails with attached images to download, and it could lock up a slow dial-up connection for hours. Here's a better way.

If you place your photos on your website, and tell your friends about them, they can visit in their own time. And if you organise the photos so that visitors can view and select from 'thumbnails', then they will only have to wait to see the images that they really want. To set this up, you would need to take each of the photos into your graphics software, resize it down to 150 or so pixels wide or high, and save it with a new name. Each full-size image is then inserted into its own web page. All the thumbnails are added to a single page, and each one will have a hyperlink to connect to its big brother. Find two or three suitable digital photo files and work through this next practice.

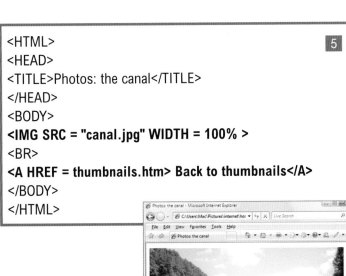

```
<HTML>                                                    [5]
<HEAD>
<TITLE>Photos: the canal</TITLE>
</HEAD>
<BODY>
<IMG SRC = "canal.jpg" WIDTH = 100% >
<BR>
<A HREF = thumbnails.htm> Back to thumbnails</A>
</BODY>
</HTML>
```

## Create the image pages

1. Take the first image file. If you want to reduce download time, resize it to fit neatly onto the screen.

2. Save the file with a name that will remind you of its content.

3. Resize the image again, reducing it to a thumbnail of 100–200 pixels width. Save this with a name that is based on the full-size image – add 'thumb' or 'mini' or a number to the end.

4. Go to your editor and start a new HTML file.

5. There are only two essential lines in the BODY area: an <IMG SRC...> tag to display the image, and a hyperlink to jump back to the thumbnails page. This doesn't exist yet, but we can still write the tag <A HREF = thumbnails.htm>...

6. Save the page file with the same name as the image file.

7. Repeat steps 1 to 6 for the other images.

# Linking a thumbnail to an image (cont.)

## Create the thumbnail page

1. Start a new HTML file.

2. Type in code along the lines shown here, changing the title, heading and filenames to suit your pages and images, and adding suitable ALT text to the images.

3. Save it as 'thumbnails.htm'.

4. Open the thumbnails file in Internet Explorer.

5. Click on a thumbnail and you should jump to the page with its full-size image.

6. Click the Back to thumbnails link to return to the thumbnails page.

7. Follow the links to the other images.

2

```
<HTML>
<HEAD>
<TITLE>My holiday snaps</TITLE>
</HEAD>
<BODY>
<H2>Photos from my French holiday</H2>
<A HREF = vines.htm > <IMG SRC = "vinesmini.jpg" ALT
= "Vines near the Dropt" > </A>
<A HREF = church.htm > <IMG SRC = "churchmini.jpg"
ALT = "The Church at La Reole" ></A>
<A HREF = canal.htm > <IMG SRC = "canalmini.jpg" ALT
= "The Canal Lateral" ></A>
<BR>
</BODY>
</HTML>
```

Notice how the <IMG SRC...> tags fit between the <A HREF ...> and </A> tags.

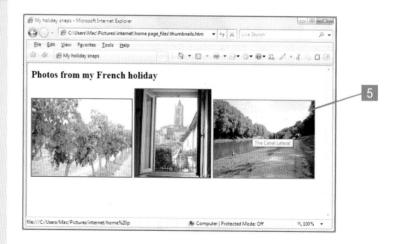

5

If you have worked through the examples so far, you should now have a dozen or so web page files. What we now need to do is link them together to turn them into a site. To do this, we will edit the index.htm file – our Welcome page – and write into it hyperlinks to the other pages. We then edit each of the second-level pages in turn, adding a hyperlink to take visitors back to the top page.

```
<HTML>                                              [2]
<HEAD>
<TITLE>Mac's web site</TITLE>
</HEAD>
<BODY>
<H1>Welcome to my site</H1>
<FONT SIZE = 5>
<A HREF = text.htm> Formatting text </A> <BR>
<A HREF = colours.htm> Colours </A> <BR>
<A HREF = fontsize.htm> Font size </A> <BR>
<A HREF = lines.htm> Lines</A> <BR>
<A HREF = lists.htm> Lists </A> <BR>
<A HREF = links.htm> Links </A> <BR>
<A HREF = images.htm> Images </A> <BR>
<A HREF = thumbnails.htm> Linked images </A> <BR>
</FONT>
</BODY>
<HTML>
```

1 Open the index.htm file in your editor.

2 Edit the file to add hyperlinks to each of the second-level pages.

3 Save the file.

4 Open the first of the other pages and add this line at the bottom of the code, just before the </BODY> tag:

   <A HREF = index.htm> Back to home page</A>

5 Save the file.

6 Repeat for the rest of the pages.

7 Open the index.htm file in Internet Explorer.

8 Use the links to open the other pages in turn, going back to the index each time.

**Important**

If your index page has an html extension, make sure you use this in the HREF at step 4.

## Adding keywords in a META tag

The META tag allows you to add information about a page, for use by search engines and directories when they add the page to their databases. On a personal website, it would only be written into the top page, and would refer to the whole site. The basic META tag shape is:

    <META NAME = … CONTENT = … >

The NAME can be a range of things, including:

- keywords, for indexing by search engines

- description, which some search engines and directories will use when listing your site.

The CONTENT is any appropriate text. For keywords it can be a series of words or "phrases in double quotation marks", separated by commas, e.g. if someone used their site to organise and advertise their local pigeon fancying club, the top page should have a tag like this:

    <META NAME = keywords CONTENT = "racing pigeons",
    "Grimsby Feathers Club", Humberside, races, birds>

1. Open your index.htm file.

2. Add two new lines into the HEAD area, and type in the <META … tags for keywords and description. Follow the structure shown here, but with your own content.

3. Save the file.

4. Open the file in Internet Explorer. You should not see any change at all – if there is something different, then there must be something very wrong with one or other of the new tags!

```
<HTML>
<HEAD>
<META NAME = keywords CONTENT = McBride, "Pearson
Education", HTML, "web pages", samples, brilliant>
<META NAME = description CONTENT = "Sample web
page files from Brilliant Internet">
<TITLE>Mac's web site</title>
</HEAD>

<BODY>
…                                                    2
```

Your website isn't actually a website until it's up on the web, and that means copying the files onto your designated place at your Internet service provider's site. Exactly how the place will be configured, and how you get your files there varies. The basic process is always the same – files are uploaded using FTP (File Transfer Protocol) which is the most efficient way to move files around the Internet. But some ISPs have very simple uploading routines, with the FTP facility built into their web pages. Others expect you to get your own FTP software and manage the job by yourself. If, like me, you have one of those ISPs, here's how to upload files using an FTP program. This is Core FTP, but they all work in much the same way.

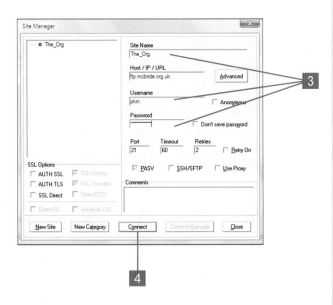

# Uploading your files

1  Get the necessary details from your ISP. You will need to know the URL of the host computer – the place where your files are stored, your login name and password. You will also need to know the URL of the home page of your site.

2  Start your FTP software. If this is the first time that you have used it, it will probably take you directly to the routine to set up host.

3  Enter the URL of the host computer, your user name and password. Leave the other settings at their defaults unless your ISP has specifically told you the settings to apply.

4  Click the Connect button.

# Uploading your files (cont.)

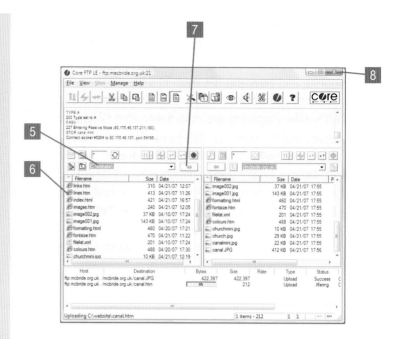

5   If the details are correct, and the connection is made successfully, you should be returned to the main window of your FTP software. The pane on the left relates to your computer, that on the right to the host. On your computer, navigate to the folder that contains your website files – you may need to experiment to find the way to change folders in your software.

6   Select the files to be uploaded. For selecting multiple files, the usual [Ctrl] and [Shift] techniques will work.

7   Look for a button to start the upload – it may be labelled, or simply have an arrow pointing to the host pane. Click it, and wait for a response. You should get a progress report as files are transferred.

8   When all your files are uploaded, exit from the software.

9   Run Internet Explorer, and type in the URL of your site. Do you get your home page? Do the links work? Do things look as you had expected?

You can produce web pages in Word – and you don't have to think about which tags to use. You write and format the page more or less as you would any other Word document, using the normal tools. The only difference is that you save it in web page file format. Word replaces its own formatting and layout codes with HTML tags, and outputs a standard HTML text file.

Note the 'more or less' back there. Web pages are different from documents produced for printing, and this has a little impact on the way that you work in Word. The first thing to note is that web pages are not a fixed shape – they are not A4!

■ It helps if you start a new file using the Blank Web Page option.

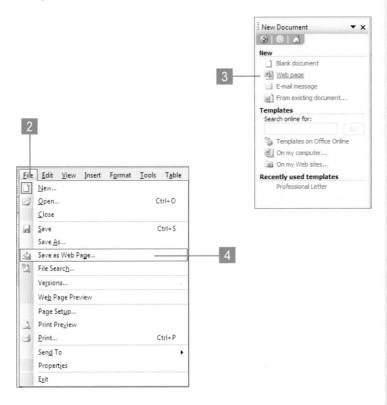

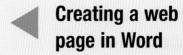
1 Open Word.

2 If the New Document task pane is not visible, open the File menu and select New…

3 Select Web page from the New options.

4 Open the File menu and select Save as Web Page…

## Important

When you are creating any document – not just web pages – it is good practice to save a file immediately, even though it is still blank. This sets the file name and the file format. While you are working on it, you should resave it regularly – and all you need to do then is click the Save button.

# Creating a web page in Word (cont.)

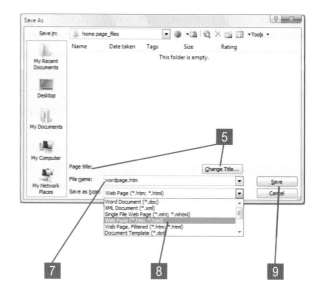

5 If there is a heading in the page, this will be offered as the Page Title. If not, or if you don't want the suggested title, click Change Title... .

6 Enter the title and click OK .

7 Edit the suggested File name or enter a new one.

8 Set the Save as type to Web Page.

9 Click Save .

HTML formatting is more limited than normal Word formatting. Most tools can be used happily, though some options can raise problems.

Fonts are best left alone. If you use any other than the standard ones – Times New Roman, Arial and Wingdings – there's no guarantee that other people will have them on their PC, so your page may not look the same to them.

Similarly, borders, highlights and changes in the font size, may not be displayed properly on some browsers.

1 Type your text as normal. When formatting, use:

the Styles for headings;

Bold and Italic for emphasis;

the Left, Right and Centre buttons to set alignment;

the numbered and bulleted lists buttons to create UL and OL lists;

the text colour button.

2 Save the file regularly.

3 Open the file in Internet Explorer to check its appearance. It should look very similar to how it is in Word.

Styles   Bold   Italic   Centre   Left   Right   Numbered list   Bulleted list   Text colour

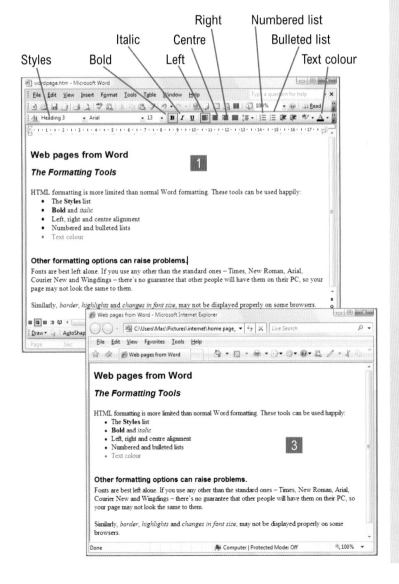

# Creating a link in Word

Word has a simple routine for creating hyperlinks, though it has one little oddity that you must be aware of. When you write the address into the dialogue box, if it doesn't start with 'www…' you must type 'http://' before the address. For example, to link to the main BBC site you could use www.bbc.co.uk, but to link to the News site you would have to write http://news.bbc.co.uk.

1 Select the text or the picture that is to carry the hyperlink.

2 Click 🖳 the Insert Hyperlink button.

3 At the Insert Hyperlink dialogue box, check that the Text to display is correct.

4 Type in the Address, preceded by 'http://' if it doesn't start with 'www'.

5 Click OK .

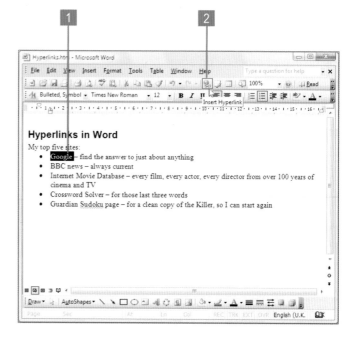

## Did you know?

Hyperlinks can be written into any kind of Word document – not just web pages.

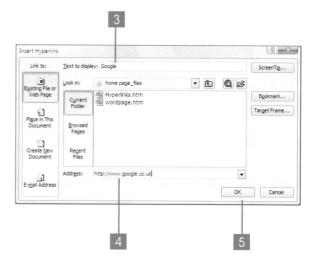

As well as creating hyperlinks in Word, you can also start browsing from them, and although you are no longer in Word when you do that, Windows software is so integrated that you will switch to Internet Explorer in the same window and may not even notice it!

Simply clicking or double-clicking on a hyperlink in Word does no more than if it were plain text. But if you hold down [Ctrl], a click will activate the link.

1 Go online if you are not already connected.

2 Hold down [Ctrl].

3 Point to the text or image carrying the link – a tip box will appear showing the linked address.

4 Click to go. The Word window will become an Internet Explorer window, and the linked page will be displayed.

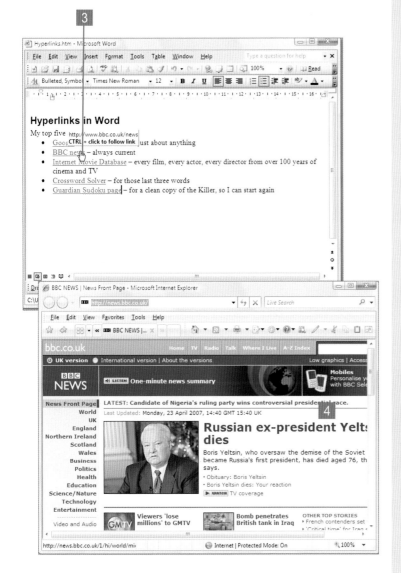

# Jargon buster

**Bandwidth** – strictly refers to the capacity of the phone line, but is also used to refer to other transmission and storage resources. If someone describes your email or your website as being a 'waste of bandwidth', they didn't think much of it!

**Browse** – move from one site to another on the web, enjoying the scenery and following up leads. Also called surfing.

**Browser** – application specially designed for accessing and displaying the information in the World Wide Web. This is also true the other way: the web is an information system designed to be viewed on browsers.

**Domain name** – the part of an Internet address that identifies the organisation that it belongs to.

**Email** – electronic mail, a system for sending messages and files across networks.

**Error-checking** – techniques used to make sure that data sent over the Internet arrives intact. If a block of data is damaged, it is sent again.

**File transfer** – download documents and files from special file stores.

**Flames** – bad tempered emails, typically sent by the more aggressive members of a newsgroup when someone has made a particularly stupid or unacceptable remark.

**Freeware** – software available for free download. Just because it is free does not mean it is no good.

**Googling** – search the Internet for information; generally, but not necessarily, at Google.

**Host computer** – one that is permanently connected to the Internet and which provides storage space for files that others can access, or manages email or offers some other service.

**HTML** – HyperText Markup Language, a system of instructions that browsers can interpret to display text and images. HTML allows hypertext links to be built into web pages.

**Image map** – picture with several hyperlinks attached to different areas, so that the one picture can be the route to many places.

**Internet** – the global network of computers, linked by cables and microwave links, and the software systems that allow them all to interact.

**Internet service provider** – organisation whose main business is to enable people to access the Internet.

**ISP** – see Internet service provider.

**Lurking** – reading, without posting – so that you can get a feel of what a newsgroup is about.

**Mail server** – computer that stores and handles email.

**Meta-information** – information written into HTML pages for the benefit of spiders, but not visible on screen.

**Mirror** sites – ones that holds the same files, organised in exactly the same way as at the main site. Many popular file stores have mirror sites.

**Net** – short for Internet. And Internet is short for interlinked networks, which is what it is.

**Page** – or web page, a document displayed on the web. It may be plain or formatted text; and may hold pictures, sounds and videos.

**Plain text** – text without any layout or font formatting.

**Portal** – website that aims to be central to how people use the web, by providing a range of services and activities, such as a directory, search facility, games, email and chat rooms.

**rot13** – a simple coding system that substitutes each letter with the one 13 along (wrapping round from Z back to A). It hides the meaning of a message from casual glances. There is an Unscramble option on the Message menu if you need it.

**Shareware** – software that can be tried for free for a limited time. To continue using the software, you need to register and pay the fee (typically around £30).

**Shouting** – writing messages or newsgroup articles entirely in capitals. Not a good idea as they are harder to read.

**Site address** – the identifier of the website. This will be a main part of the addresses of pages at that site or of people who get their email through the site.

**Snail mail** – hand-delivered by the postman.

**Spam** – unsolicited emails, all trying to part you from your money in one dodgy way or another, sent out in huge numbers.

**Surfing** – following links to move from one web page to another, at the same or a different site.

**Telnet** – running programs on a distant computer, something purely for the techies.

**Thread** – a series of replies to an article, and the replies to the replies, and so on…

**Web** – World Wide Web. Also shortened to WWW or W3.

**Web host** – organisation that provides a web address and the space to store the files, so that people and smaller firms can set up their own websites.

**Web page** – the basic web document. It may just be a single screenful or you may have to scroll down to read it all.

**Website** – a set of related pages, usually owned by one organisation or individual. Visitors will arrive at the top level page, which will usually act as a kind of contents list, carrying links to the other pages within the site.

**World Wide Web** – the most visible and one of the simplest and most popular ways of using the internet. It consists of billions of web pages, which can be viewed through browsers

**Zip files** – files compressed by WinZip. if you have Windows Vista or XP, you can open these in Windows Explorer, which treats them as compressed folders. If you have an older version of Windows, you will need a copy of WinZip to extract them. Self-extracting Zip files have the unpacking routines built into them.

# Troubleshooting guide

## Multimedia

## Newsgroups

## Searching

## Windows Mail: using

## Windows Mail: customising

## Web pages: viewing

# New! Features

## Microsoft Windows Vista

Microsoft Windows Vista has a brand new user interface that makes it easier and faster to use than earlier versions of Windows. Tasks such as opening and closing applications, searching for files and changing settings have been streamlined. New and improved programs have been developed to help you manage and store pictures, send and receive emails, browse the Internet, backup your data and stay secure. And the flexible new interface allows you to customise toolbars and optimise your working environment using Sidebars and Gadgets.

## What's New?

The **New!** icon in the table of contents highlights the sections that have been significantly revised to demonstrate how tasks are carried out in the new Vista operating system. The following lists all the significantly revised and new sections and their location in the book.